THE
S·C·E·N·T·E·D
HOUSE

*A creative guide to fragrant and decorative ideas
for every room in the house*

THE
S·C·E·N·T·E·D
HOUSE

A creative guide to fragrant and decorative ideas
for every room in the house

❧ PENNY BLACK ❧

Photography by Geoff Dann

DORLING KINDERSLEY · LONDON

In memory of my darling mother, whose passion for cottages and gardens has become my own.

Important Notice
The recipes in this book are perfectly safe when properly mixed.
However, some of the ingredients may cause allergic reactions in some
individuals so reasonable care in the preparations is advised.

A DORLING KINDERSLEY BOOK

ART EDITOR CAROLINE MULVIN
PROJECT EDITOR JO WEEKS
MANAGING ART EDITOR ALEX ARTHUR
MANAGING EDITOR JANE LAING

First published in Great Britain in 1990 by Dorling Kindersley Limited
Henrietta Street, London WC2E 8PS
Reprinted with revisions 1991

British Library Cataloguing in Publication Data
Black, Penny
The Scented House
1. Handicrafts using scented plants
I. Title
745.92
ISBN 0–86318–485–5

Typeset by The Cooling Brown Partnership, Hersham, Surrey
Reproduced by Colourscan, Singapore
Printed and Bound in Italy by A. Mondadori, Verona

CONTENTS

INTRODUCTION

Of all the five senses there is none that stimulates the imagination more than that of smell. The subconscious memory is steeped in perfume and the merest drift of scent can evoke vivid recollections of sensations long since forgotten. More than all others it is the familiar scents of childhood that capture our imagination and transport us back to those early years. Who can smell a garden after summer rain without basking in its comforting sweetness? And who cannot find solace in the scented flowers of dusk and night?

❀ FLOWER ARRANGEMENTS *Dried flower arrangements can be large and flamboyant (right) or small and subtle (above). They are always an attractive decoration for the home.*

My own childhood memories are infused with the rich smells of the country and through them I am taken back to Dorsetshire fields, woods and hedgerows, to our garden and the humble little thatched cottage where I lived. In the woods nearby lingered the seductive Eastern perfume of honeysuckle, whose pale, nectared flowers so beguilingly projected their fragrance at the close of the day.

✧ BLUEBELLS & PRIMROSES ✧

There were juicy-stemmed bluebells, whose evocative sweet perfume is reminiscent of blue skies and warm summer sun, and delicate pallid primroses, whose mossy scent is the language of childhood. On dry banks grew aromatic cushions of thyme and in the water-meadows watermint guarded her secret fragrance until her downy leaves were trampled upon. In the garden grew heady lilac, clove-scented rambler roses and aromatic lad's love. Lily-of-the-valley filled shady corners and provided sweet white bells to perfume nosegays and buttonholes. Inside the cottage scented

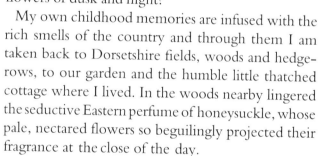

smoke from burning apple logs, oil lamps and beeswax candles hung in the air, the tangy aroma of boiling marmalade and fresh mint sauce often filled the kitchen and from the medicine chest came the vaporous smell of friar's balsam and camphorated oil. On warm summer nights the exquisite perfume of jasmine drifted gently through my bedroom window.

For thousands of years fragrant flowers, leaves, roots, seeds, woods and resins have been used to scent our homes, food, clothes as well as ourselves. As we gradually became aware of the soothing and sybaritic properties of perfume, more sophisticated means were found to capture the many aromas of the natural world.

✧ THE ORIGINS OF PERFUME ✧

It was probably the scented smoke of burning wood that first alerted our senses to the pleasure of perfume for the word "perfume" is derived from *per fumin*, meaning "by means of smoke".

The Egyptians were the first to record the art of perfumery and it became an integral part of their everyday life. The perfumed resins of frankincense and myrrh were burned as fragrant offerings to the gods and the temples were heavy with their sweetness. With the discovery that many aromatics possess both germicidal and preservative properties, embalming, or mummification, became part of the Egyptian burial ritual. Scented cedar wood was used in the making of coffins, and the dead were buried with a fascinating array of fragrant unguents and oils. Elaborately perfumed preparations were massaged into the body and scented cosmetics

were used to rejuvenate and enhance facial beauty; there were even recipes for primitive deodorants. Bowls of scented botanicals perfumed rooms, as did burning incense. Frankincense, myrrh, sandalwood, calamus, cassia, cinnamon, peppermint, juniper, henna, orris and sweet herbs are just a few of the aromatics that were used. All of them are familiar and found in many of the recipes in this book. Many of them were carried to Egypt by Ishmaelite traders who ran the gauntlet of the ancient caravan routes to trade their spices and resins in the Land of the Pharoahs.

✧ PERFUME IN EUROPE ✧

The civilizations of the ancient Western world gained their knowledge of perfumery through the Egyptians. The Greeks often referred to perfume in their writings on mythology and all of their religious ceremonies involved the burning of incense and herbs. Highly fragrant cosmetics were used and herbal medicine was practised.

The Romans learnt the aesthetic appreciation of scent and the art of perfumery from the Greek colonists of southern Italy. Following the fall of the Roman Empire European interest in perfumery declined and only the Christian church preserved the ancient rituals of incense burning and those that involved the use of fragrant oils. During the Dark Ages it was the monasteries that cultivated aromatic flowers and herbs, but not for the use of making perfumes, rather for preparing herbal remedies and medicines.

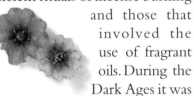

✧ THE PERFECTION OF DISTILLATION ✧

However, during this period, the Arabs continued their research into the properties of fragrant plant materials and in the eleventh century the Arabian doctor Avicenna perfected the science of distillation.

❋ SCENTED DECORATION *The fragrant winter-leaf pot pourri in the patchwork cushion (above) will fill the living room with an intriguing perfume. The lovely bedroom garland (left), hung over a bed-post, will imbue the room with a delicate scent.*

Avicenna distilled the "attar", or essential oil, from the rose. This oil remains the most historic and important essential oil and is known as the "attar of roses".

✧ THE CRUSADERS & PERFUMERY ✧

The Crusaders revived the lost art of perfumery in Europe when they returned from the eastern Mediterranean, bringing with them many exquisitely perfumed toiletries and exciting new aromatics.

By the sixteenth century most large houses grew herbs and scented flowers – particularly roses – in their gardens. They were gathered by the mistress of the house and taken to her "still-room" – a room apart from the kitchen where a stove kept the atmosphere warm and dry. They were dried and stored there together with the many imported herbs and spices that were available. Oils, fats and lards, lanolin, beeswax and precious animal fixatives added to the fascinating contents of the room. One can imagine the delectable and curious scents that filled the air. Here the housewife dispensed all the cosmetics, cleaners and medicines that were essential to the well-being of her family and the sweetness of her home.

✧ ROOM SWEETENERS ✧

Large bundles of herbs were prepared for strewing on the floors and fumigating the rooms. Scented pastilles and incense cones were made to sweeten the air, as were rich moist pot pourris. Fragrant and moth-repellent fillings were made for sachets, which were then used to perfume and protect clothes and linen. Aromatic pomanders and spikenard, rosemary and lavender beads were fashioned from gums, resins, fixatives and essential oils; they perfumed the air and their germicidal properties helped to ward off infection. Delicately scented washballs, soaps, colognes, floral waters, oils and other preparations were made for cosmetic use.

❧ EXOTIC AROMATICS ❧

With the advancement of scientific research many changes took place in the world of perfumery between the seventeenth and twentieth centuries. The scents of the fragrant flowers, leaves, woods and spices of the New World became more readily available: rhodium, cascarilla, sassafras, allspice, balsam of Peru, tonquin and vanilla are a few of the poetically named aromatics from the Americas and West Indies. French and British perfumers of the nineteenth century sold an incredible assortment of fragrant colognes, soaps, pomades and oils, hair dyes and depilatories.

The twentieth century brought many changes, including the introduction of chemical fragrances, and gradually the diversity of the perfumer's preparations diminished. Pot pourri, scented sachets and natural-beauty products temporarily fell out of fashion as we became reliant on artificially scented products. Today, however, we are once again eager to perfume our homes and ourselves with the lovely natural fragrances that captivated our ancestors.

❧ THE ROSE ❧

Look to the Rose that blows about us – "Lo, Laughing," she says, "into the World I blow: At once the silken tassel of my Purse Tear, and its Treasure on the Garden throw"
From the Rubaiyat of Omar Khayyám

The unique role of the rose in perfumery has been, and remains of immense importance. The Egyptians adored it and it was sacred to their Goddess Isis. The fragrance of the rose contributed to their religious and domestic perfumery and was so much in demand that they exported roses made from fragments of wood, paper and cloth, after scenting them with rose oil. The Greeks and the Romans used the perfume of the rose in

❀ CHAIR CUSHION *In the filling of this lovely cushion (above), spicy, woody and floral scents are blended to produce a wonderful perfume.*

oils, unguents and essences and its petals were strewn on floors, used to fill mattresses and pillows and scattered on the living and over the tombs of the dead. Rose water even played in their fountains! In this book roses or rose oil are used in most recipes. The "rose leaves" referred to in many recipes in the old herbals are actually rose petals.

❧ ESSENTIAL OILS ❧

Essential oils are found in all aromatic plant materials: they give the flowers, leaves, seeds, roots, woods, resins and balsams their fragrance. Distillation is the most usual method of separating the oils from the plant materials. During this process the plant materials are saturated with steam from boiling water, making their fragrant oils evaporate. The resulting vapour mixes with the steam, and as the steam condenses the oil separates from it and floats on the surface. It can then be collected and bottled.

Another method of removing fragrant oils is extraction. This involves infusing the botanicals in either a fixed solvent of fat or oil, or a volatile solvent such as ether. Oils may also be obtained by expression, whereby pressure is applied to the leaves and flowers to squeeze out the oils.

The names of most essential oils are straightforward; here are some that are more misleading: *Neroli* – from the blossoms of the sweet orange, *Petitgrain* – from the twigs and leaves of the bitter orange tree, *Orange* – from the peel of the bitter orange, *Bergamot* – from the peel of the bergamot orange, *Bergamot mint* – from the leaves of the bergamot mint, *Monarda* – from the flowers and leaves of bergamot (*Monarda didyma*), *Ambrette* – from musk seeds.

❧ FIXATIVES ❧

Fixatives play an essential role in perfumery, for they fix or hold, the fragrance of the volatile essential-oils contained in the scented plant materials. Without fixatives perfume quickly loses its fragrance. Fixatives are often aromatic and their scent will add to the bouquet of a perfume.

Fixative properties are found in certain gums, resins, flowers, leaves, roots, seeds, spices, herbs and even lichens. In this book I have used orris root powder or finely ground gum benzoin because they are readily available. But you can use oakmoss, crumbled cinnamon sticks, sweet Cicely, angelica, coriander and cumin seeds, crushed tonquin beans, chopped roots of sweet flag and elecampane, crumbled leaves of melilot or woodruff and finely ground resins of myrrh, galbanum and labdanum. If a dry fixative is not appropriate, oil of sandalwood, clove, cassia, cedarwood or patchouli may be used.

✤ A MEDLEY OF SCENTED DELIGHTS ✥

The Scented House is filled with both traditional and innovative ways of perfuming every room in the house. Some of the fragrant delights are steeped in antiquity, whilst others are my own ideas. Any natural, absorbent material can easily be impregnated with

❧ LAVENDER BASKET *(above) Decorations of pink and white flowers emphasize the beautiful simplicity of this display of mainly blues and greys.*

scent, giving immense scope to the field of creative perfumery. I use dried plant materials as an exciting medium with which to create intricate botanical embroideries and patchworks. The fragrance of a summer garden pervades the pressed- and dried-flower collages, while the aroma of herbs and the sweet fragrance of the rose lingers in the stationery. I love embroidery, fine sewing and old textiles and, when making scented pillows, cushions and sachets, I always consider both their fragrance and appearance. Even the bottles that contain my colognes, oils and sweet waters are decorated with sprigs of flowers and herbs. My home is a feast of visual pleasure and all the scented accessories in this book reflect my interest in the decorative arts as well as in perfumery.

The Hall & Stairs

THE HALL SETS THE SCENE for the entire home, and what could be more welcoming than a seductive fragrance. On entering the visitor immediately searches for the source of the perfume and derives much pleasure from the discovery of a basket or bowl brimming with pot pourri, or an aromatic garland behind the door or looped over the newel post of the stairs. There are many garland bases available and when they are decorated with dried flowers, leaves, fruit, whole spices, mosses and lichen, their romantic charm always adds interest to any interior. Pretty old hats and bonnets, stuffed with sweet herbs and flowers, are a delightful decoration. One used to be able to obtain scented pictures from the East, with hollow frames which were filled with spicy aromatics. Although these are no longer available you can easily recreate them by rubbing wooden picture frames with the essential oil of cloves, cinnamon, nutmeg, sandalwood or cedarwood. Gentle, subtle perfumes are best for the hall and stairs as they will not spread to overwhelm the scents in other rooms. Colours should be warm and welcoming. The browns of woods and spices and the subdued pinks, mauves and blues of cottage garden flowers are ideal. Aromatic woods can often be collected on a woodland walk. Fir needles are easily discovered as are conifer foliage and fir cones, the refreshing scent of which can be strengthened by dropping a little pine oil into their centres. Sharpen woody scents with the intriguing perfume of bergamot orange. The shadowy fragrance of the rose is always welcome. Mix it with sweet herbs to produce a very lovely traditional fragrance.

❀ GARLANDS & COLLAGES *Unusual garlands (left) and delicately-scented collages (above) are wonderful decorations for the hall and stairs.*

❧ FLORAL HOOPS ❧

CONSIDER CAREFULLY the colours and scents to use in your floral decorations for the hall, as they will be the first decorations a visitor to your house will encounter and they are therefore bound to make a significant impression. Shades of brown and green and woody or spicy scents are ideal as they empathize with the world outside, so close at hand. If you have also made pot pourris for the hall, ensure that their scents and colours complement those of the garlands. In addition to the wall, you might also like to hang a garland on the newel at the end of the banisters or on the inner side of the front door. Enhance or refresh the scent of a garland by rubbing perfumed oil into the willow base or by periodically spraying the base or the flowers with perfume.

LILAC

POTENTILLA

✿ SEMI BASKET *Flowers and other plant materials, scented with essential oils and glued to a cardboard backing, produce a fine display for this two-dimensional garland.*

EVERLASTING FLOWERS

ROSE

❀ MOSSY GARLAND
*Browns, creams, greys
and greens are used to
give this garland a
muted appearance. A
lovely scent is produced
by the sandalwood oil, which
has been dropped on the
oakmoss and the pine cones,
and the whole spices.*

FIR CONE

CINNAMON STICK

WHEAT EAR

NUTMEG

❀ DELICATE CIRCLET
*Rose oil and myrrh oil
have been dropped into
the centre of each of
the roses to imbue this
dainty circlet with a
wonderful perfume
that is both ancient
and evocative.*

SEA CARROT

GLOBE AMARANTH

✿ SCENTED BASKET
*This beautiful dried-
flower display, arranged
in an aromatic, vetiver
basket has an unusual
fragrance of orange and
frankincense.*

✿ SHOE CLEANING BOX
*Painted matt-black and
edged with gold leaf, this
unusual container is
filled with a rich and
spicy Elizabethan
pot pourri of roses
and herbs.*

✿ INGREDIENTS
(LEFT): ANAPHALIS (DYED
PINK), DOUBLE DAISY,
GYPSOPHILA, LARKSPUR,
POTENTILLA, ROSE,
ROSE BUDS,
ROSE PETALS
AND VERBENA.

❧ POT POURRIS ❧

Woody scents are particularly appropriate for the hall, making a gentle transition from the outside to the inside world. Old-fashioned domestic containers, such as tea caddies, biscuit barrels, sewing boxes, chocolate boxes, hat boxes and even shoe boxes, can be used for displaying pot pourri, often with marvellous results. Use the hall table, the floor, the stairs, the wall or a coat hook to present your pot pourris.

❀ INGREDIENTS (LEFT): ABUTILON, LAVENDER, LILAC, MALLOW, POTENTILLA, ROSE, ROSE PETALS AND SEA CARROT.

❀ WOODEN BOWL *The emphasis is on texture in this heady, woody pot pourri. Potentillas and delphiniums add splashes of colour.*

❀ INGREDIENTS (RIGHT): CINNAMON STICK, CLOVES, CORK SHAVINGS, DELPHINIUM, FIR CONE, NUTMEG, POTENTILLA, SENNA PODS, STAR ANISE, STAR TILIA AND WOOD SHAVING.

❧ FLORAL WALL HANGINGS ❧

THE LARGE AREA OF WALL SPACE in the hall and by the side of the stairs is ideal for the display of hanging scented decorations. Eye-catching arrangements for these positions can take almost any form you like. Try decorating objects that are usually found in the hall, such as the coat rack or the umbrella stand, or make just one bold design that will act as a focal point. As the hall and stairs are generally quite airy, make the scent fairly strong but not so powerful that it spreads throughout the rest of the house and overwhelms the perfumes in other rooms. Woody scents are very effective or, for a refreshing fragrance, try mixing citrus peel and herbs.

❀ HEART OF HOPS
& HEATHER
*Visually stunning,
although simple in
design, this rich
purple and pale green
heart is scented with a
pot-pourri reviver.*

✿ POSY OF PRESSED FLOWERS *This tiny, pressed-flower bouquet is bordered with a gilt frame. The back of the frame has been rubbed with oil of cloves, so that the picture exudes a strong but simple fragrance.*

✿ EDWARDIAN HAT *Decorated with dried flowers and filled with pot pourri, this lovely hat exudes the rich fragrance of scented woods and bergamot orange.*

❧ RECIPES ❧

POT POURRIS FOR DISPLAY

SWEET MIX

*

1 litre (2pt) Mixed Scented
Flowers
60g (2oz) Rosemary
30g (1oz) Orris Root Powder
1/2 Chopped Vanilla Pod
2 Tonquin Beans
2 Teaspoons Grated Nutmeg
2 Drops Carnation Oil
2 Drops Neroli Oil
2 Drops Rosemary Oil

*This sweet but subtle dry pot
pourri is lovely in the
hall and stairs
area.*

WOODY MIX

*

500ml (1pt) Mixed Scented Woods
500ml (1pt) Mixed of any of the
following – Berries, Cork
Shavings, Fir Cones, Nutmegs,
Senna Pods, Star Tilia Flowers
30g (1oz) Rosemary
30g (1oz) Orris Root Powder
3 Cinnamon Sticks
3 Star Anise
4 Tonquin Beans
3 Drops Cedarwood Oil
3 Drops Sandalwood Oil
1 Drop Frankincense Oil
Pink Potentilla
& Blue Delphinium
Flowers to Decorate

*The **Wooden Bowl** (p.17)
displays this woody-scented
dry pot pourri, which is ideal
for the hall. It has a heady
fragrance that is strong
enough to perfume
a large area but is
not too pervasive.*

ELIZABETHAN MIX

*

1 litre (2pt) Mixed Pink & Blue Flowers
60g (2oz) Mixed Sweet Herbs
30g (1oz) Lavender
30g (1oz) Fine-ground Gum Benzoin
2 Teaspoons Crushed Allspice Berries
1 Teaspoon Cloves
1 Crumbled Cinnamon Stick
4 Drops Elizabethan Pot-pourri Oil
2 Drops Clove Oil
Woodrush Flowerheads to Decorate

*The **Shoe Cleaning Box** (p.16) is filled
with this old-fashioned dry pot pourri. It is
a lovely mix, ideal for filling the hall and
stairs area with a gentle scent.*

✺ Woody Mix *The most suitable
pot pourris for the hall and stairs
are those that contain woody
ingredients. This mix is perfect
as it combines the lovely warm
colours and textures of woody
pine cones, nutmegs, star
anise and star tilia with the
brighter colours of potentilla
and delphinium flowers.*

TANGY ROSE MIX

500ml (1pt) Mixed Whole Roses
& Rose Petals
500ml (1pt) Mixed Garden Flowers
30g (1oz) Lemon Verbena
30g (1oz) Lavender
30g (1oz) Orris Root Powder
2 Teaspoons Cinnamon Powder
1 Teaspoon Cloves
1 Teaspoon Coriander Seeds
4 Drops Orange Oil
2 Drops Frankincense Oil
Bunch of Lavender to Decorate

*The **Scented Basket** (pp.16-17) displays this dry pot pourri. The orange and frankincense oils lend it a deep, tangy fragrance that is sweetened and softened by the roses.*

FIR CONE MIX

1 litre (2pt) Mixed Fir Cones
2 or 3 Small Citrus Pomanders
(optional)
30g (1oz) Lavender
30g (1oz) Fine-ground Gum Benzoin
1 Chopped Vanilla Pod
2 Teaspoons Allspice Berries
4 Drops Juniper Oil
2 Drops Lemon Oil
2 Drops Orange Oil

This is a lovely highly textured dry pot pourri, ideal for displaying in the hall and stairs area.

AUTUMN BERRY & LEAF MIX

500ml (1pt) Brightly Coloured
Autumn Leaves (gathered
before they fall & very
lightly pressed for
2 or 3 days)
500ml (1pt) Mixed Hips,
Haws & Berries
30g (1oz) Lavender
30g (1oz) Fine-ground
Gum Benzoin
4 Tonquin Beans
2 Broken Cinnamon Sticks
1 Teaspoon Cloves
4 Drops Rhodium Oil
2 Drops Myrrh Oil
2 Drops Rose Oil

The lovely bright colours of autumn are captured in this dry pot pourri.

POT POURRIS FOR CONTAINERS

BERGAMOT ORANGE & SANDALWOOD MIX

500ml (1pt) Sandalwood Shavings
500ml (1pt) Bergamot Leaves
60g (2oz) Lavender
30g (1oz) Orris Root Powder
Grated Rind
of an Orange
2 Teaspoons Crushed
Allspice Berries
1 Teaspoon
Cinnamon Powder
4 Drops Sandalwood Oil
2 Drops Bergamot Oil

*The **Edwardian Hat** (p.19) is stuffed with this dry pot pourri. Bergamot orange and sandalwood combine to produce a delicious fragrance. Fill the crown of the hat with the pot pourri. Keep it in place with a circle of net, slightly larger that the base of the crown, loosely tacked in place.*

THE LIVING ROOM

Of ALL THE ROOMS in the house, the living room is the best place to display your most lavish perfumed achievements. Pressed-flower pictures, using the scented flowers of a summer garden or an array of old roses, surrounded by a mixed border of flowers, are lovely. Use scented paper as a base or perfume the flowers so that the air around the collage is infused with fragrance. If you have the space, a large basket filled with fascinating aromatics might make the most intriguing feature in the room. Be imaginative when displaying pot pourri. Bowls, jars, dishes and baskets of fragrant mixes can be placed almost anywhere. Create immense impact by filling an old wooden rocking cradle, a chest or a dough bin with a magnificent display of dried roses, peonies, tulips and any other rich and flamboyant flowers. Make appliqué and

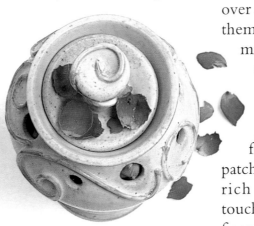

✿ MIXED FRAGRANCES *A large dried-flower bouquet (left) or a diffuser full of moist pot pourri (above) will fill the room with a lovely blend of scents.*

patchwork cushions and sachets from scraps of fabric and lace, or create frilled and piped cushions from a fabric that matches or co-ordinates with the other soft furnishings in the room. If the fragrant delights are to be displayed over a large area, scent them with different mixes, although be careful not to make them too overpowering. Just a little myrrh frankincense or patchouli will add a rich and soothing touch to the lighter fragrances of lavender, geranium, rose and tangy orange. The perfumes of fragrant woods and seeds have a unique softness that blends well with almost all other scents. Of course, you may well prefer to use quite different perfumes in your living room than those suggested. It is all a matter of personal choice, and you can have great fun experimenting to discover what appeals most.

❧ CUSHIONS ❧

SWEETLY PERFUMED cushions are a delightful way to scent the living room. Use pretty scraps of linen, lace and fabric to make opulent appliqué cushions or more humble patchwork ones – whichever suits the room. Fabrics that co-ordinate with other soft furnishings are also appropriate. Choice of scent is highly personal and can vary from light perfumes to luxuriant aromas.

❀ PATCHWORK & APPLIQUE
These lightly scented, handworked cushions are ideal for cottagey rooms.

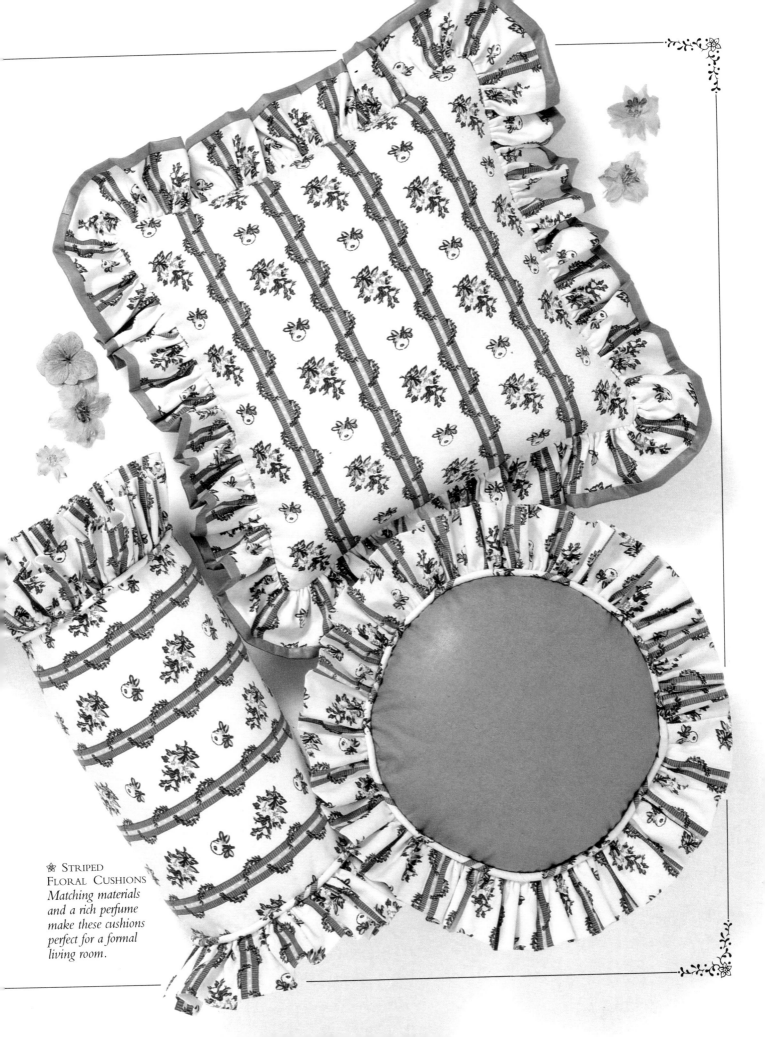

❀ STRIPED
FLORAL CUSHIONS
*Matching materials
and a rich perfume
make these cushions
perfect for a formal
living room.*

✤ PATCHWORK SQUARES
*These square sachets,
carefully trimmed with
lace and ribbon, and
filled with a sweet wood
pot pourri, should be
displayed in a
prominent position
where their intricate
designs can be seen
to advantage.*

✤ AROMATIC
HEART *Filled with
mixed aromatic seeds,
this rich red heart makes a
lovely, luxurious decoration.*

☙ PETITE SACHETS ➳

SMALL SACHETS, filled with herbs and scented mixes, will fill the living room with a subtle fragrance. Suspend them from small hooks on the bookcase, doorknobs, radiators, curtain rails and curtain ties; tuck them into the sides of chairs and sofas; or lay them on a flat surface, such as a coffee table. Wherever you place them, they are bound to be appreciated for their delicate appearance and their intriguing fragrance. Make individual sachets using small scraps of material remaining from other projects, or use the same material as the cushions to make an attractive set of colour-coordinated soft furnishings. Even fragile laces and silks can be used if backed with iron-on interfacing. The shape you choose to make your sachets is a matter of individual preference. Size is also dependent on taste but be sure that they are small enough to be dainty and elegant. Try making several tiny sachets and link them together on a wooden ring, or make a larger sachet and decorate it with embroidery or lace.

❀ TUBULAR POUCHES *A pair of slim sachets, exuding a woody rose scent are perfect for placing in drawers.*

❀ SPHERICAL SACHETS *These little bags hang together on a fine wooden ring to make an unusual decoration, suitable for tying to the end of a curtain rod.*

❀ APPLIQUE LACE BAG *Trimmed with delicate, cream lace, this little bag exudes a fragrance of orange and patchouli.*

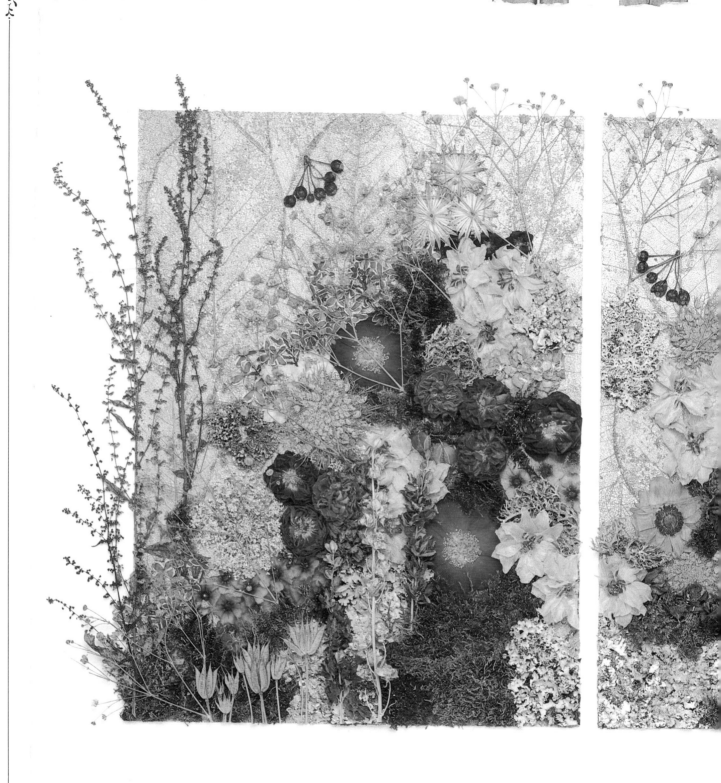

❧ GARDEN COLLAGE ❧

ELEGANT, SCENTED, PRESSED-FLOWER COLLAGES provide a delightful way to perfume a room gently as their shadowy fragrance is distinct only when you pass close by. To make the most impact, large collages must have plenty of wall space; smaller collages are less dominant and look delightful displayed with other pictures. You can make these pictures almost exclusively from aromatic botanicals, although it is sometimes preferable to scent the paper before starting on the design. Alternatively, if you are using a wooden frame, you might like to rub an essential oil into the back.

— CREATING A COLLAGE —

Creating a collage presents endless possibilities. Almost any pressed plant material can be used: mosses, lichens and fungi, weeds, herbs, spices, fruits, berries and seedheads, all garden flowers and even some seaweeds. Aromatic, whole spices, such as cloves, produce lovely, textural contrasts and add to the bouquet of the picture. Dried botanicals are subtly coloured, so it is possible to mix many different hues without the risk of their clashing.

— FINDING INSPIRATION —

Inspiration can come from your own garden, or from anything that is ornamented: china, embroidery and textiles, paintings and illustrations, jewellery and even a sheet of gift wrapping paper. Recreate a summer flower border using elements in the way that they appear naturally, or try making your own abstract and geometric designs.

❀ SUMMER BORDER *Skeletonized leaves, sprayed silver-blue, are the perfect backdrop for this lovely design. A drop of rose geranium oil, then a drop of clary sage oil is put in the centre of each rose and the lichen is scented with 3 drops of frankincense oil. The resulting fragrance is nostalgic and cottagey.*

❧ SINGLE ARRANGEMENTS ❧

IN THE LIVING ROOM, large and solitary aromatic arrangements are very effective, especially when displayed in a prominent position. If your living room is spacious and sparsely furnished, a large display will accentuate its elegance and grandeur, while a single, eye-catching but small-scale decoration can provide a small room, which may have a tendency to feel overcrowded, with the illusion of space. In large rooms, where space is not a problem, display your creation on the floor or on a side table, or make it the centre of a larger display, surrounding it with smaller, complementary decorations. If you decide to create a large arrangement for a small living room, ensure that there is enough space to set it off and make it a focal point. A basket arrangement looks superb placed on the floor by the fireplace or on a windowsill.

— COLOURS —

It is not essential to choose strong, sharp colours when creating large arrangements for the living room as their size alone will ensure that they are eye-catching. A very striking idea is to use mainly subtle or muted colours but also to include one or two brighter colours in order to lift the display.

— SCENTS —

Depending on taste, scent can range from the simple to the sophisticated. Often large decorations are most effective if the fragrance is fairly light but comprises a mixture of perfumes.

❀ BASKET OF
FRAGRANCE *This
basket is filled with a
delectable assortment of
plant materials, including
bundles of cinnamon sticks,
lavender twigs, orris root,
driftwood scented with essential
oil, and several types of fir cone.
The various elements are arranged in
informal groups, thus emphasizing the
contrasts of colour, texture and shape. The
whole basket exudes a bouquet of subtle perfumes.*

❧ POT POURRIS ❧

IN THE LIVING ROOM, many surfaces can be used for displaying pot pourri, including coffee tables, bookshelves, floors and window-sills. The range of scents is also wide. Decide what sort of atmosphere you wish to produce and then give your creativity a free rein. Try unusual colour combinations like sea-green and slate-blue, and experiment with different textures, such as papery, satin-smooth roses combined with rough fronds of lichen.

❀ INGREDIENTS: ANAPHALIS, HYDRANGEA, LARKSPUR, OAKMOSS AND WATER FORGET-ME-NOT.

❀ LITTLE BLUE VASE *The strong perfume of rose and frankincense permeates through the decorative top layer of this moist pot pourri.*

❀ INGREDIENTS: ANAPHALIS (DYED PINK AND JADE), GYPSOPHILA, LAVENDER, DAMASK ROSE AND PEACH ROSE.

❀ ALMOND-GREEN BOWL
In this pot pourri (left) the brown of the cinnamon blends with the pink of the roses, and the grey-green of the oakmoss matches the bowl. The scent is a light fragrance of mint and rose.

❀ DECORATIVE ISLAMIC BOWL
An Eastern influence is clear in the colour scheme of this mix, from the Damask rose in the centre to the dyed jade anaphalis around the edge. The scent is suitably oriental, combining tea tree oil with piquant geranium oil.

❀ INGREDIENTS: CINNAMON STICKS, OAKMOSS, *ROSA MUNDI, ROSA* 'FELICITE PERPETUE' ROSE BUDS AND RUGOSA ROSES.

❧ SCENTED STATIONERY ❧

PRESSED FLOWERS, glue and good-quality art paper are all that you require to make your own unique and charming cards, notelets, note paper, envelopes, bookmarks and gift tags. Perfume your stationery by storing it in a small box or a drawer along with a sachet of pot pourri. Choose one of your favourite scents to perfume the paper and alter it whenever the mood takes you. Bookmarks can be scented with woodruff, which is an insect-repellent and is a time-honoured protector of paper. Scent your inks with a fragrant infusion – the traditional perfume is patchouli – for a personal touch to your letters.

❀ PEN & INK
Scent your ink with heady patchouli.

❀ CARDS & NOTELETS
These beautiful cards are imbued with the scent of a lavender sachet and decorated with pressed flowers.

❀ WAXED CARDS *Rose-scented wax scents and protects the pressed flowers on these cards.*

✿ BOOKMARKS *Woodruff decorates and scents the bookmark on the right, that on the left has a spicy clove perfume.*

✿ GIFT TAGS *These tags are perfect for a special gift.*

✿ NOTEPAPER & ENVELOPES *Make matching writing paper, using one or two pressed flowers. Sandalwood perfumes this paper.*

 RECILPES ❧

POT POURRIS FOR CUSHIONS

FRAGRANT WINTER-LEAF MIX

1 litre (2pt) Mixed Scented Leaves from the Winter Garden such as Bog Myrtle, Box, Conifer Tips, Eucalyptus, Hypericum, Jerusalem Sage, Myrtle & Pine Needles
60g (2oz) Rosemary
30g (1oz) Orris Root Powder
2 Teaspoons Cloves
2 Broken Cinnamon Sticks
6 Drops Myrtle or Pine Oil
2 Drops Rosemary Oil

*The **Patchwork & Appliqué Cushions** (p.24) are filled with this light, fresh dry pot pourri, which is ideal for filling cushions.*

SPRING NOSEGAY MIX

1 litre (2pt) Mixed Scented Spring Flowers such as Hyacinths, Jonquils, Lilies-of-the-Valley & Violets
60g (2oz) Lavender
30g (1oz) Orris Root Powder
2 Teaspoons Crushed Mace
Peel of $1/2$ an Orange
Peel of $1/2$ a Lemon
2 Drops Jonquil Oil
2 Drops Lavender or Violet Oil
2 Drops Lily-of-the-Valley Oil

*The **Striped Floral Cushions** (p.25) are stuffed with this rich dry pot pourri that will fill the living room with the scent of spring.*

❋ Applique Lace Bag
This attractive appliqué lace bag exudes the heady fragrance of the Patchouli, Jasmine & Orange Mix.

POT POURRIS FOR SACHETS

WOODSIE ROSE MIX

500ml (1pt) Rose Petals
500ml (1pt) Mixed Scented Woods
30g (1oz) Lavender
30g (1oz) Ambrette Seeds or Chopped Eryngium Roots
2 Teaspoons Crushed Coriander Seeds
2 Tonquin Beans
4 Drops Rose Oil
2 Drops Cedarwood Oil

*The **Tubular Pouches** (p.27) are filled with this dry pot pourri. The delicious musky fragrance of this mix is lovely in the living room.*

SWEET WOOD MIX

1 litre (2pt) Mixed Scented Woods such as Barberry Bark, Cedarwood, Cinnamon Bark, Cypress Wood, Logwood Chips, Quassia Chips, Santal Wood, Sandalwood, Sassafras & Fragrant Sawdust
60g (2oz) Lavender
30g (1oz) Fine-ground Gum Benzoin
2 Teaspoons Crushed Allspice Berries
4 Star Anise
4 Drops Bois de Rose Oil
4 Drops Cypress Oil

*The **Patchwork Squares** (p.26) are filled with this pervading woody-scented dry pot pourri, which is ideal for sachets.*

AROMATIC SEED MIX

1 litre (2pt) MIXED AROMATIC SEEDS
SUCH AS ALLSPICE, AMBRETTE,
ANGELICA, CARAWAY,
CARDAMOM, CORIANDER,
CUMIN, NUTMEG, STAR ANISE,
SWEET CECILY & TONQUIN BEANS
60g (2oz) ROSEMARY
30g (1oz) ORRIS ROOT POWDER
30g (1oz) CINNAMON POWDER
6 DROPS AMBRETTE,
ANGELICA OR CLARY SAGE OIL
2 DROPS COSTUS
OR VIOLET OIL

*The **Aromatic Heart** (p.26) and
the **Spherical Sachets** (p.27) are
filled with this dry pot pourri, which
has a spiced musky fragrance
strengthened by sweet violet oil.*

PATCHOULI, JASMINE & ORANGE MIX

875ml (1³/₄pt) JASMINE FLOWERS
125ml (¹/₄pt) ORANGE PEEL
60g (2oz) LAVENDER
30g (1oz) ORRIS ROOT POWDER
1 CHOPPED VANILLA POD
1 TEASPOON GRATED NUTMEG
4 DROPS JASMINE OIL
2 DROPS PATCHOULI OIL

*The **Appliqué Lace Bag** (p.27)
contains this dry pot pourri. The
jasmine and patchouli in this luxuriant
mix produce a heady scent, which is
sharpened by the tangy orange peel.*

❋ PATCHWORK
SQUARE *Filled
with Sweet Wood
Mix, this sachet is
perfect for displaying
in the living room.*

POT POURRIS FOR DISPLAY

ELEGANT ROSE MIX

500ml (1pt) MIXED WHOLE ROSES
500ml (1pt) OAKMOSS
60g (2oz) DRIED MINT
30g (1oz) ORRIS ROOT POWDER
1 TEASPOON CRUSHED MACE
4 TONQUIN BEANS
4 BROKEN CINNAMON STICKS
PEEL OF A LEMON
3 DROPS ROSE OIL
1 DROP LEMON OIL
1 DROP PEPPERMINT OIL

*The **Almond-green Bowl** (p.33)
displays this traditional dry pot
pourri. Its scent is sweet but refreshing.*

ORIENTAL GERANIUM MIX

1 litre (2pt) MIXED SCENTED FLOWERS
60g (2oz) SCENTED GERANIUM
(PELARGONIUM) LEAVES
30g (1oz) FINE-GROUND GUM BENZOIN
2 TEASPOONS CINNAMON POWDER
¹/₂ GRATED NUTMEG
PEEL OF ¹/₂ AN ORANGE
PEEL OF ¹/₂ A LEMON
4 DROPS TEA TREE OIL
2 DROPS GERANIUM OIL
1 DROP PATCHOULI OIL
JADE- & PINK-DYED ANAPHALIS
& WHOLE ROSES TO DECORATE

*The **Islamic Bowl** (p.33) contains
this dry pot pourri, which has an
intriguing oriental fragrance.*

HERBAL MIX

1 litre (2pt) STOCK-POT PETALS
60g (2oz) MIXED SWEET HERBS
30g (1oz) LEMON VERBENA
30g (1oz) OAKMOSS
30g (1oz) ORRIS ROOT POWDER
1 TEASPOON CINNAMON POWDER
1 TEASPOON CLOVES
1 TEASPOON GRATED LEMON RIND
4 DROPS GERANIUM OIL
2 DROPS FRANKINCENSE OIL
BLUE FLOWERS TO DECORATE

*The **Little Blue Vase** (p.32) contains
this rich and evocative moist pot pourri.*

SCENTED INK

PATCHOULI INK

250ml (¹/₂pt) PATCHOULI LEAVES
375ml (³/₄pt) BOILING WATER

*Patchouli Ink (p.34). Place leaves and
water in a bowl. Leave for 2 hours
then strain into a pan. Boil until the
liquid is reduced by half. When cool,
add 1 teaspoon to 60ml (2fl oz) of ink.*

The Kitchen

❋

Most kitchens enjoy a cornucopia of sweet-smelling ingredients. Cloves, cumin, allspice, coriander and many other spices are used extensively in today's cosmopolitan cuisine, as are many sweet herbs including marjoram thyme, sage and mint. Their delicious fragrance can also be used selectively in almost every pot pourri, not to mention pomanders, collages and dried-flower displays. Try using more unusual aromatics, such as eucalyptus and myrtle leaves, lemon verbena, bergamot, feverfew, catmint and fluffy heads of Joe Pye weed, in kitchen pot pourris, together with tangy citrus fruits. Shining brass and copper containers evoke the atmosphere of the kitchens of the past and look gorgeous crammed full of sweet-smelling, freshly-picked herbs and perhaps some bunches of immature fruit.

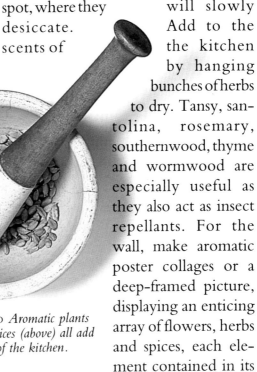

❋ Fresh & Dried *Aromatic plants (left) and crushed spices (above) all add to the aromas of the kitchen.*

Alternatively, place an ample trug, laden with herbs and flowers in a warm, dry spot, where they will slowly desiccate. Add to the scents of the kitchen by hanging bunches of herbs to dry. Tansy, santolina, rosemary, southernwood, thyme and wormwood are especially useful as they also act as insect repellants. For the wall, make aromatic poster collages or a deep-framed picture, displaying an enticing array of flowers, herbs and spices, each element contained in its own compartment. Lastly, there are few things more pleasurable at the end of the day than the intimacy of a meal at the kitchen table under the soft, honeyed glow of fragrant candles. Ideal kitchen colours are verdant greens, bright yellows and oranges, red and the essential dash of blue.

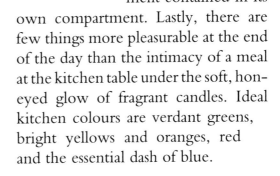

❋

❧ GATHERING FLOWERS & HERBS ❧

WHEN YOU HAVE SPENT TIME nurturing the herbs in your garden, it is infinitely satisfying to be able to collect some and bring them into the house so that you can continue to appreciate them when it is not possible to be outside. The best time to gather most herbs is in late summer when they are mature but have not yet begun to deteriorate. Evergreen herbs, such as rosemary and thyme, can be harvested at any time of the year, although it is best to allow new growth to harden before winter sets in. If you are picking the herbs for their leaves, it is best to do this in the morning immediately after the sun has evaporated the dew; gather the flowers at midday when they are fully opened.

— USING HERBS —

Arrange some fresh herbs in an attractive container to decorate the kitchen and to be within easy reach when they are needed for culinary or medicinal purposes. Hang herbs that are not wanted for immediate use in bunches in a shady part of the room. Later they can be added to scented mixes or they can be crumbled and stored in jars for use in cooking in the winter.

❀ BUNCH FOR HANGING
*Two varieties of feverfew –
single- and semi-double-
flowering – together with
Bowles' variegated apple-
mint make up this simple
herbal bouquet secured with
raffia. The yellow centres of
the feverfew flowers are
pretty when dry. If the
mint is to be used in
cooking it should
be picked before it
flowers.*

❀ TRUG OF HERBS
*A trug is ideal for
collecting flowers and herbs.
It has a flat base, which allows
the plant material to lie together
loosely without being crushed, and it
is shallow, so the air can circulate
around the plants, keeping them
fresh until you are ready to remove
them. This attractive, rustic trug is
filled with eupatorium, bergamot,
marigolds, alchemilla, smallage,
sweet flag and artemisia.*

❧ FRESH HERB DISPLAYS ❧

SHINING BRASS AND COPPER KITCHEN CONTAINERS are perfect receptacles in which to arrange herbs. Here the interesting textures and lovely brilliant greens of the herbs contrast strongly with the smooth, metallic sheen of the kettle, jug and ship's water canister. A large number of these old-fashioned herbs, such as marjoram, smallage and fennel, are useful for flavouring food. Some have other household uses – feverfew can be employed for medicinal purposes, soapwort is a washing agent and artemisia, when dried and crumbled, is a good moth repellant.

❀ SHIP'S WATER CANISTER
This unusual dispenser (right)
is filled to overflowing with a
wonderful assortment of plant
material including astrantia,
bistort, crab apples, double
chamomile, euphorbia, fennel,
feverfew, fleabane, Inula
hookeri, I. magnifica,
marjoram, meadowsweet,
Polygonum campanulatum,
St John's wort, smallage
and variegated mint.

❀ COPPER JUG *Meadowsweet, fennel, soapwort, bergamot, smallage, astrantia, double chamomile, verbena, feverfew and* Inula hookeri *combine to create a striking arrangement in this bright copper jug (below left).*

❀ BRASS KETTLE *Containing stems of euphorbia, lemon balm, vervain, good King Henry, garden rue, lad's love, St John's wort, royal fern and purple sage, this brass kettle (below) is a charming vessel for such a display.*

☙ BOTANICAL POSTERS & SAMPLERS ❧

INTRIGUING AND BEAUTIFUL POSTER COLLAGES are easily made using the basic elements of perfumery. These basic elements include herbs, spices, gums, resins, seeds and barks, many of which are used in the kitchen, so it is the most appropriate room in which to display collages of this kind. Try producing a formal arrangement of herbs and spices, annotating the poster in the manner of an old botanical illustration. Another possibility is to take the delightful needlework samplers of the eighteenth and nineteenth centuries as your inspiration, and create a display of pressed and scented flowers, herbs and whole spices, berries and lichen. The fragrance produced by these posters is a subtle blend of the elements that have been used. If you wish to make the perfume more pronounced, scent the paper before you begin the design.

❀ TRADITIONAL DESIGNS
This herb poster (left) is annotated, giving it a traditional, botanical appearance. The lavish collage (right) is designed to be like a needlework sampler with plant materials replacing the embroidery stitches.

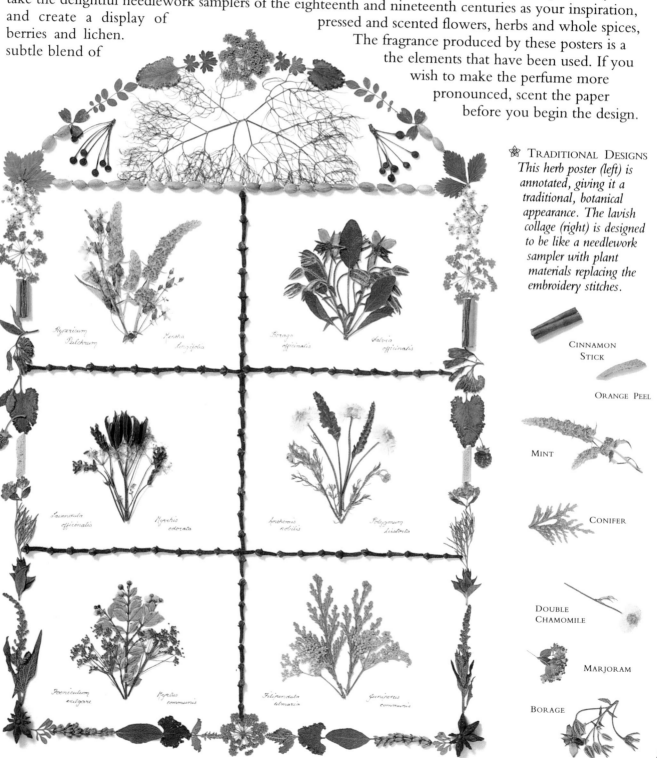

CINNAMON STICK

ORANGE PEEL

MINT

CONIFER

DOUBLE CHAMOMILE

MARJORAM

BORAGE

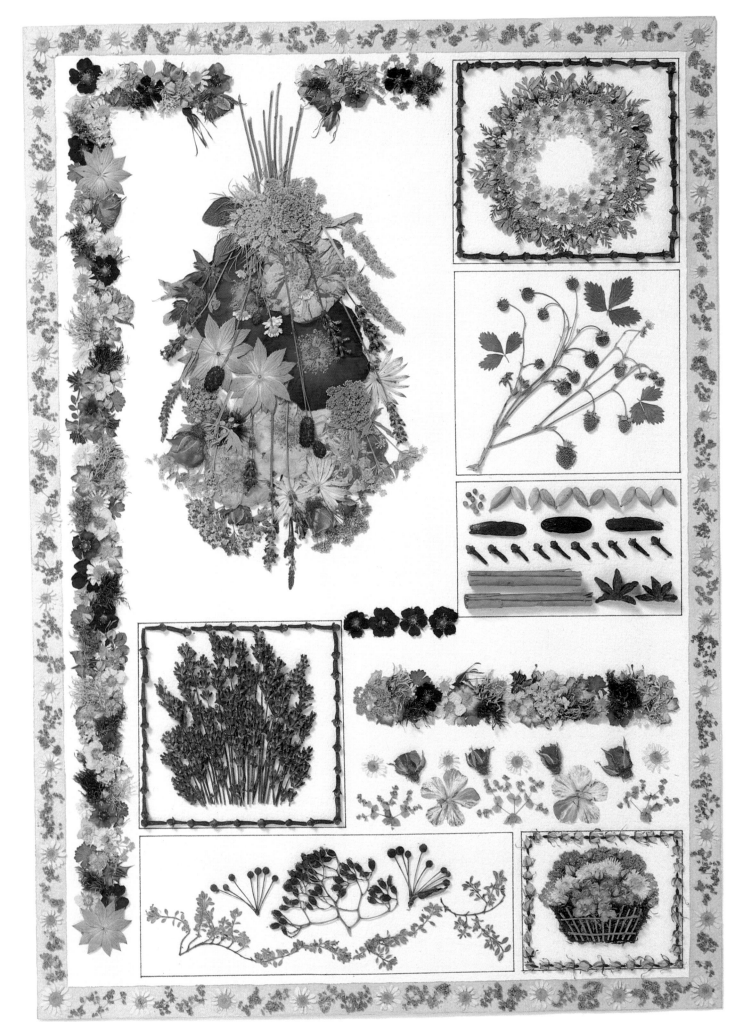

❧ BOLD DISPLAYS ❧

BOLD BUT SIMPLE SHAPES look stunning in the kitchen whether displayed singly or in groups, on the windowsill, the dresser or even the kitchen table. You can make a wonderful, self-contained decoration with just a few basic, kitchen-related elements. Alternatively, by using a wealth of plant material of many different hues, you can build up a tremendously exuberant and eye-catching display. Designs for the kitchen should always be bright and cheerful so the best colours to use are shades of orange, red, yellow and green. The most suitable scents for these displays are strong, but clean and crisp, and, once again, associated with the kitchen. Spicy or fruity fragrances, for example, will blend in with cooking smells and refresh the kitchen when preparations for the meal are complete.

✿ CITRUS POMANDERS
Oranges, lemons and grapefruit pierced with cloves exude a refreshing and tangy scent. Ribbons, beads and several undecorated fruits complete the arrangement.

❀ VETIVER BELL
Made of vetiver,
which has a persistent,
sweet aroma, this bell is
filled with a beautiful display
of dried plant materials,
including achillea, fir cones, roses,
Doronicum and mosses. The
nutmeg and cinnamon sticks relate
the design to the kitchen and the warm
colours ensure the arrangement is eye-catching.

❧ NATURAL STORES ❧

KITCHEN DECORATIONS can range from the incredibly simple to the very complicated with infinite variations in between. Decorations need not be traditional; indeed you can be as innovative as you wish. However, when creating a display for the kitchen, remember to include some elements in your design that are related to cooking or food and be sure not to overestimate the available space. Small kitchens are easily overwhelmed with the everyday clutter of cooking, so if your kitchen is tiny make small and simple decorations that will brighten dark corners. For a sizeable kitchen, you can be more adventurous and create a large, imposing arrangement. As with the size of the design, the strength of the perfume should vary in accordance with the size of the kitchen. A large, old-fashioned or draughty kitchen will require a stronger perfume than a small, modern, fitted kitchen.

❀ CORN SACK
Filled with cloves and decorated with wheat ears and cinnamon sticks, this tiny sack exudes a spicy fragrance.

❀ SCENTED STORE
This wooden frame contains fragrant herb and spice mixes as well as flowers, in a formal design. The delicious scent of the pot pourri seeps through the wood.

NUTMEG

ORANGE PEEL

ROSEMARY

CLOVES

CARDAMOMS

❀ BRASS BOWL *Originally used for skimming cream, this bowl displays the sharp, citrus-yellows of the mix to perfection. A vibrant contrast is provided by the violet-blue mallows. The perfumes of lemon balm and rosemary pervade this mix.*

❀ SLIPWARE DISH *In this pot pourri, spices, flowers, herbs, seedpods, seedheads and citrus peel combine to produce an interesting texture as well as to provide a brightly coloured display and a delicious perfume of citrus and marigold.*

MARSH MARIGOLD

COCKSCOMB

MALLOW

POTENTILLA

STAR ANISE

SCABIOUS

EVERLASTING FLOWERS

CINNAMON STICK

EVERLASTING FLOWERS

DORONICUM

ACHILLEA

OAKMOSS

ORANGE PEEL

POTENTILLA

SENNA PODS

GRASS SEEDHEADS

❧ POT POURRIS ❧

POT POURRIS FOR THE KITCHEN should have a strong, fruity, herby or spicy scent to cut through the cooking smells, so often prevalent there, without clashing with them. Use food containers, such as jelly moulds, bargeware, dinner plates and bowls, and oven dishes to emphasize further the relationship between the pot pourris and the kitchen. For a subtle effect, decorate the mixes with plant material of complementary colours; for a more vivid display use flowers of contrasting colours. You can achieve an interesting effect by decorating a mixture with plant material specifically used in the kitchen – seeds, herbs and spices are all suitable. Stand completed arrangements on the table, dresser or windowsill, or try putting one in a hanging basket and suspending it from a beam. Avoid placing pot pourris on busy work surfaces, where they may be in the way, or close to the cooker and its accompanying steam, which will cause the scent to deteriorate quickly.

❋ SCARLET BASKET *This rich blue pot pourri contrasts strongly with the scarlet basket. Coriander adds a spicy touch to the herb-scented mix.*

LARKSPUR

LAVENDER

CINNAMON
STICKS

❧ BURNING PERFUME ❧

CANDLES IN THE KITCHEN evoke a nostalgic, rustic atmosphere. Eating by their mellow light transforms any meal into a special occasion, and the atmosphere is made more memorable if the candles are scented. Candles in the kitchen can be perfumed with herbs, oils and essences, or perhaps the unique, honeyed fragrance of beeswax is the most appealing. Single candles are lovely displayed in traditional holders or on saucers, although table candelabras, holding several tapering candles, will provide more light. An intriguing mixture of perfumes is produced by grouping an assortment of tiny, fragrant candles on a plate. Night lights can be placed in a perfume vaporizer where they will produce a muted light and a strong scent as the perfume evaporates.

❀ MATCHING HERB CANDLES
These candles are all decorated with old-fashioned, cottage-garden herbs. They are scented with lemon balm, thyme, rosemary and bergamot.

❀ HEART-SHAPED CANDLE
This peppermint-scented candle (left) is decorated with borage.

❀ DAINTY CANDLES *Tiny candles (left) are pretty when clustered on a plate.*

❀ BAYBERRY
CANDLES *These
simple and pleasing
candles are scented
with bayberry essence.*

❀ BEESWAX
CANDLES *The rich,
honeyed scent of
these candles adds
to their charm.*

❀ PERFUME VAPORIZER
*The bowl of perfume is placed
above the lighted candle and the heat
from the candle causes the perfume to
evaporate, so creating a pervading aroma.*

ꙮ RECIPES ꙮ

POT POURRIS FOR DISPLAY

SPICY LEMON MIX
*

1 litre (2pt) Mixed Blue Flowers
30g (1oz) Orris Root Powder
1 Finely Crushed Cinnamon Stick
2 Teaspoons Allspice Berries
4 Drops Clove Oil
4 Drops Geranium Oil
4 Drops Lemon Oil

*The **Scented Store** (pp.48-9) is filled with this dry pot pourri. Three of the compartments contain pot pourri, decorated with blue flowers. To add to the bouquet of the pot pourri the other compartments are filled with lavender, rosemary, nutmegs, cardamoms, cloves, citrus peel, fir cones and oakmoss. When putting the pot pourri in the compartments, be sure to cover it with pretty flowers. This is for decoration and also because it contains orris root powder, which will cloud the glass if it comes in direct contact with it. Hang the picture in a warm place so that the scent is stronger.*

❀ Pestle
& Mortar
Fresh, crushed herbs fill the kitchen with a lovely aroma.

HERB & SPICE MIX
*

1 litre (2pt) Blue Larkspur Flowers
60g (2oz) Mixed Sweet Herbs
30g (1oz) Fine-ground Gum Benzoin
2 Teaspoons Caraway Seeds
1 Teaspoon Coriander Seeds
Peel of a Lemon
4 Drops Coriander Oil
2 Drops Lemon Oil
Little Bundle of Cinnamon Sticks, Lavender & Larkspur Spikes to Decorate

*The **Scarlet Basket** (p.51) is filled with this dry pot pourri in which fragrant herbs and spices are carefully blended to produce a subtle bouquet.*

CITRUS & MARIGOLD MIX
*

500ml (1pt) Mixed Yellow & Orange Flowers
500ml (1pt) Lemon Verbena
30g (1oz) Mixed Sweet Herbs
30g (1oz) Oakmoss
30g (1oz) Senna Pods
30g (1oz) Orris Root Powder
2 Teaspoons Cinnamon Powder
2 Broken Cinnamon Sticks
Peel of ¹/₂ an Orange
Peel of ¹/₂ a Lemon
4 Drops Marigold Oil
2 Drops Orange Oil
1 Drop Lemon Oil
Yellow Doronicum Flowers & Seedheads to Decorate

*The **Slipware Dish** (pp.50-1) contains this dry pot pourri. The ingredients blend to produce a beautiful display as well as a captivating perfume.*

SPICE MIX
*

500ml (1pt) Mixed Whole Spices – such as Allspice Berries, Cardamoms Cinnamon Sticks, Cloves, Coriander Seeds, Juniper Berries, Nutmegs & Star Anise
500ml (1pt) Mixed Seedheads – such as Aquilegia, Clematis, Hellebore, Love-in-a-Mist, Poppy, Sea Carrot & Wheat Ears
30g (1oz) Lavender
30g (1oz) Fine-ground Gum Benzoin
4 Drops Vetiver Oil
2 Drops Lavender Oil
2 Drops Lemon Oil

This beautifully textured and brightly coloured dry pot pourri is ideal for displaying in the kitchen.

GERANIUM & LEMON MIX

500ml (1pt) BLUE
LARKSPUR FLOWERS
500ml (1pt) LEMON VERBENA
60g (2oz) LAVENDER
30g (1oz) FINE-GROUND
GUM BENZOIN
1 TEASPOON CARAWAY SEEDS
1 TEASPOON
CORIANDER SEEDS
1 TEASPOON CLOVES
4 DROPS GERANIUM OIL
2 DROPS LEMON OIL

*The geranium oil in this dry
pot pourri produces quite a musky
perfume, which is sharpened by
the lemon verbena and spices.
The colour mixture of blue and
green is lovely in the kitchen.*

❋ HERBS & POMANDERS *The bright
colours and invigorating aromas of a
bunch of fresh herbs (below) and a
tangy pomander (above right) are
delightful in the kitchen.*

LEMON & ROSEMARY MIX

1 litre (2pt) MIXED YELLOW FLOWERS
60g (2oz) LEMON BALM LEAVES
30g (1oz) ROSEMARY
30g (1oz) ORRIS ROOT POWDER
2 TEASPOONS ALLSPICE BERRIES
1 TEASPOON CUMIN SEEDS
PEEL OF A LEMON
4 DROPS MELISSA
(LEMON BALM) OIL
2 DROPS ROSEMARY OIL
BLUE FLOWERS TO DECORATE

*The **Brass Bowl** (p.50) displays
this brightly coloured dry pot pourri.
It is wonderful in the kitchen
as its overall scent is lemony.*

CITRUS PEEL MIX

1 litre (2pt) MIXED CITRUS PEEL
30g (1oz) MARIGOLD FLOWERS
30g (1oz) ROSEMARY
30g (1oz) FINE-GROUND
GUM BENZOIN
2 DROPS LEMON OIL
2 DROPS MARIGOLD OIL
2 DROPS ORANGE OIL
2 DROPS TANGERINE OIL

*This dry pot pourri is a lovely
blend of tangy citrus fruit
and heady marigold.*

BURNING PERFUME

MUSKY ORANGE

10 DROPS ORANGE OIL
2 DROPS FRANKINCENSE OIL

*The **Perfume Vaporizer** (p.53)
is burning this deliciously scented
mix. Pretty ceramic vaporizers
are available from many gift
shops. Small nightlights are
used to vaporize the perfume
in the saucer, which is placed
over the light. The nightlight
need only be burnt for 5 or
so minutes as the perfume
will continue to vaporize
after it is snuffed out.
Experiment with
different fragrant oils
to discover your
favourites.*

SCENTED CANDLES

With practice scented candles can be made
at home. However, I advise reading a book
on the subject before starting. Be careful,
as wax is highly flammable.

*Make scented candles by infusing sprigs
of dried or fresh herbs in wax heated in
a double saucepan to 82°C (46.5°F) for
about half an hour. Remove the herbs and
make the candles either by using moulds or
by dipping. Finely chopped fresh or dried
herbs can also be scattered through the
candle for decoration.*

PERFUMING WAX

360g (12oz) WAX
6 DROPS CANDLE PERFUME

*Slowly add perfume to the melted wax so
that it distributes evenly throughout. Special
candle perfumes are best but essential oils
can be used. Make the candles by using
moulds or by dipping.*

COLOURING CANDLES

WAX CRAYONS OR SPECIAL WAX
COLOURING DISCS

***Bayberry Candles** (p.53). Slowly add
colouring to the melted wax. Add bayberry
essence and make the candles as above.*

The Dining Room

Whether you have a dining room that is elegant and sophisticated or informal and cottagey, you can perfume it in many delightful ways. Like the banqueting halls of ages past, you can strew the floors with sweet-smelling herbs, although the concept might prove a little overwhelming in the smaller rooms of this day and age! A better idea may be to recreate the pot pourris of our ancestors by gathering the same materials from the garden as they did, mixing them with spices and finally adding the precious essential oils. Make sure that the fragrance is not too strong, so that the appetising aromas of the food can be savoured. The soft and gentle perfumes of lavender, roses, heliotrope, geranium and lemon verbena are perfect as they remain in the background and only manifest their fragrance

❀ Scented Linen *Napkins (above) and tablecloths are imbued with gentle fragrances by storing them with scented sachets in a linen press (left) or dresser.*

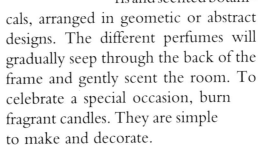

when there is no other to compete with. Create pretty, perfumed sachets and cushions that reflect the colours of your dining room or an intricate and sumptuous table centrepiece. Look for inspiration for designs in decorative china, embroidery and even fragile lace doilies. Make the most of the subtle colours and fascinating textures of dried botanicals. Arrange tiny bouquets to adorn napkin rings or place settings or large displays to loop over chair backs, all redolent with gentle perfumes. Design deep-framed collages using a variety of pot pourris and scented botanicals, arranged in geometic or abstract designs. The different perfumes will gradually seep through the back of the frame and gently scent the room. To celebrate a special occasion, burn fragrant candles. They are simple to make and decorate.

❧ POT POURRIS ❧

THE DINING-ROOM table is the ideal surface for displaying a large pot pourri as a centre-piece. Add small, matching posies to each place setting to complete the overall look. Make sure that the scent is not so overwhelming that it impairs your enjoyment of the food – light, floral or tangy fragrances are ideal.

✾ SMALL BOWL
In this informally arranged pot pourri, the traditional scent of lavender and roses is sharpened by the addition of orange peel.

STAR ANISE

ROSES

LAVENDER

ACHILLEA

BLUEBELLS

AZALEA

BLUE LARKSPUR

COLUMBINE

WHITE LARKSPUR

CLOVES

KESU

GLOBE AMARANTH

SEA CARROT

ROSE BUD

MOCK ORANGE BLOSSOM

WATER FORGET-ME-NOT

CINNAMON STICK

OAKMOSS

✾ WHITE DISH *The formal appearance of this pot pourri is accentuated by the lines of cinnamon sticks. A sweet and tangy scent of bergamot orange is softened by a hint of lavender.*

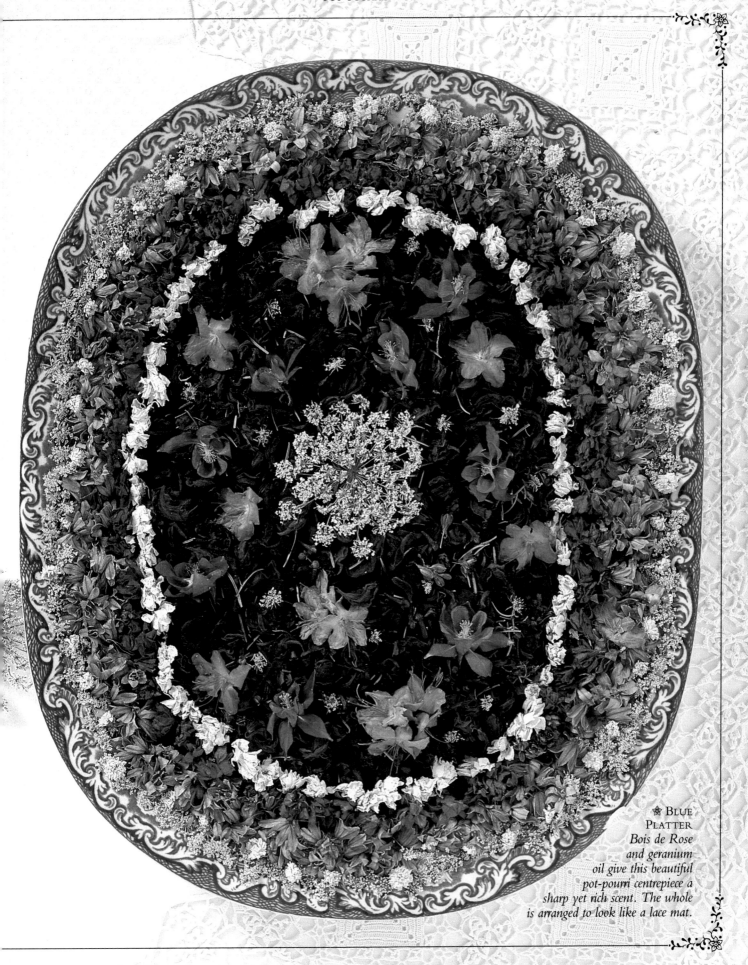

❀ BLUE
PLATTER
*Bois de Rose
and geranium
oil give this beautiful
pot-pourri centrepiece a
sharp yet rich scent. The whole
is arranged to look like a lace mat.*

❀ RED WINE *Wine has
a pleasing bouquet, which
adds to the ambience
of an evening meal.*

❀ POPPYSEED ROLL
*Fresh bread has a
wonderfully
appetising aroma.*

TABLE DECOR

SCENTED DECORATIONS for
the dining-room table
make an important dinner
party or romantic evening
meal even more special.
Matching posies for
each place setting are
very effective. Alter-
natively, if you feel
adventurous, a floral
centrepiece of dried
flowers looks stunning.
If you also perfume the
napkins and tablecloth, ensure
that the fragrance of the floral
decorations complements them.

❀ FLORAL CENTREPIECE
Beautifully made with rose
buds, roses, globe amaranths,
sea carrot and larkspur, this
flower-scented decoration
(above) looks perfect
placed in the centre
of the dining table.

❀ LILAC NAPKIN
Store delicately
scented sachets
with napkins
and tablecloths to
imbue them with
a gentle perfume.

❧ AROMATIC FOOD ❧

THERE ARE many plant materials that can be used to enhance the appearance, flavour and fragrance of food. Herbs and spices are reknowned for their flavoursome properties; less well known is that flowers can be used in a similar way. The lovely shapes and colours of flowers make them ideal for decorating sweet dishes and their scent adds a delicate flavour. Try making everyday foods, such as butter and sugar, more exciting by garnishing and flavouring them with flowers, and decorate cakes and chocolates with crystallized flowers.

❀ ROSE–PETAL JAM
*Rose-petal jam is
delicately flavoured
and has a gentle
perfume.*

❀ FLORAL
CHOCOLATES
*Mint chocolates
decorated with
crystallized flowers
are a lovely gift.*

✿ FLOWER BUTTER
*Violets, lavender
and sweet Cicely
leaves decorate
this butter.*

✿ SCENTED SUGAR
*Store a vanilla pod
and lavender with
sugar to make a
scented sweetener.*

✿ ELDERFLOWER
CHAMPAGNE
*Elderflowers make
a wonderful,
fragrant, fizzy
champagne.*

✿ FLOWER CAKE
*This beautiful
moist sponge cake
is decorated with
crystallized flowers
for a teatime treat.*

❧ CUSHIONS & SACHETS ❧

FILLED WITH POT POURRI OR A HERBAL MIX, cushions and sachets are perfect decorations for the dining room. For cushions, make sure that the scent of the filling is not too powerful as you will need to use a sizeable amount. By contrast, sachets are so small that the mix used for them should be quite strongly scented or it will be lost. Place cushions on chair seats and suspend sachets from the backs. The possibilites for displaying sachets are endless: loop them on the drawer handles of the dresser; hang them over the radiators; or place them in the drawers of the sideboard to scent napkins and tablecloths. Cushions and sachets look especially effective if they match one another. Little dried-flower bouquets or embroidered flowers are excellent as finishing touches of decoration.

❀ CHAIR CUSHIONS
To make a cushion that is comfortable as well as sweet-smelling, place the scented mix in an envelope of wadding and insert the whole into a cushion cover.

❀ CHAIR SACHETS
Filled with a rose and geranium mix, these charming bags are lovely decorations for chair arms and backs.

❀ RED STYLE
*Lavender and
lemon verbena
fill this bag,
which is ideal
for looping on
a door handle.*

❀ SILK HEARTS
*Small, silk roses
decorate these little,
silk taffeta sachets,
which have been
filled with rose
petals.*

❀ REGENCY
ELEGANCE *A
bergamot and
lavender mix
fills these tiny
Regency silk
sachets.*

❀ FLOWER GARDEN
*This heliotrope-scented,
Victorian ribbon sachet
is decorated with a
pressed-flower collage.*

❧ FRAMED SCENT ❧

IN MANY HOUSEHOLDS regular, everyday meals are eaten in the kitchen and the dining room is reserved for special occasions. If you tend to use your dining room infrequently, make sure that the scented decorations you create for it are long-lasting as well as beautiful. Arrangements that are glazed are ideal as they retain their scent and colour for much longer than a design that is open to the air. The scent escapes slowly through the back of the picture ensuring that it will never overpower the aroma of the food. Use different pot pourris to construct an abstract design, such as the fan shown on this page, or create a still life. Always decorate the pot pourri with whole flowers so that the powdery mix does not come into contact with the glass. Three-dimensional pictures can be displayed flat on the table or dresser or hung on the wall. If you are a handy carpenter you could make a beautiful and unique table by attaching legs to the underside of the frame and covering the pot-pourri collage with strong glass.

✽ THREE-DIMENSIONAL FAN *This wooden frame is filled with pot pourri and a variety of scented botanicals to create a beautiful, fan-shaped and highly perfumed arrangement.*

SANDALWOOD

ROSE

LEMON VERBENA

FIR CONES

LARKSPUR

NUTMEG

CINNAMON STICKS

LAVENDER

CLOVES

GLOBE AMARANTH

KESU

ROSE-PETAL JAM

750ml (1¹/₂pt) FRESH WATER
500g (1lb) GRANULATED SUGAR
250g (8oz) ROSE PETALS
JUICE OF 2 LEMONS

Rose-petal Jam (p.62). Bruise the petals, discarding the white heals. Put them in a bowl, sprinkle with half the sugar and leave overnight. Dissolve the remaining sugar in a pan with the water and lemon juice. Add the petal and sugar mix and simmer for 20 minutes. Increase heat and boil for about 5 minutes until thick. Pour in jars and seal.

ELDERFLOWER CHAMPAGNE

Elderflowers impart a distinctive flavour like that of the Muscat grape.

4 litres (8pt) FRESH WATER
750g (1¹/₂lb) GRANULATED SUGAR
6 MEDIUM FLOWERHEADS OF ELDER
2 TABLESPOONS WHITE WINE VINEGAR
2 LEMONS

Elderflower Champagne (pp.62-3). Sterilize all the equipment. Dissolve the sugar in a little of the water. Squeeze juice from the lemons and cut the rind into strips. Put washed flowers in a large non-metallic container with the lemon juice and rind, sugar-water, vinegar and remaining water. Stir and cover. Leave for 5 days. Strain liquid and pour into screw-top bottles. Serve chilled.

POT POURRIS FOR CUSHIONS

REGENCY MIX

500ml (1pt) RED ROSES
500ml (1pt) MIXED CASSIA BARK
& SANDALWOOD SHAVINGS
60g (2oz) LAVENDER
30g (1oz) ORRIS ROOT POWDER
30g (1oz) CLOVES
2 TEASPOONS CINNAMON POWDER
4 DROPS ROSE OIL
2 DROPS CLARY SAGE OIL
2 DROPS SANDALWOOD OIL

The Chair Cushions (p.64) are filled with this intriguing dry pot pourri.

❧ RECIPES ❧

AROMATIC FOOD & DRINK

When gathering flowers for use in cooking make sure they are edible. Pick them when they are dry and newly opened and be sure that they are clean and free from insects.

CRYSTALLIZED FLOWERS & LEAVES

SELECTION OF EDIBLE FLOWERS
& LEAVES
LIGHTLY WHISKED EGG WHITE
CASTER SUGAR

To decorate Floral Chocolates and Flower Cake (pp.62-3). Brush egg white over the flowers and leaves. Lightly dredge with sugar. Place them on greaseproof paper on a baking sheet and dry in a very cool oven, with the door ajar, for 3 hours. Use as decoration, securing them with beaten egg white.

✿ FINGER BOWL
A slice of lemon in warm water makes a lovely rinse for hands.

POT POURRIS FOR DISPLAY

TANGY MIX

500ml (1pt) MIXED WHITE
OR CREAM FLOWERS
500ml (1pt) LAVENDER
60g (2oz) OAKMOSS
30g (1oz) ORRIS ROOT POWDER
1 TEASPOON CRUSHED
CARDAMOM SEEDS
3 TONQUIN BEANS
4 DROPS BERGAMOT OIL
2 DROPS LAVENDER OIL
WATER FORGET-ME-NOTS
& CREAM ROSES TO DECORATE

*The **White Dish** (p.58) displays
this tangy dry pot pourri.*

RICH ROSE MIX

1 litre (2pt) ROSES & ROSE PETALS
60g (2oz) MIXED SWEET HERBS
30g (1oz) FINE-GROUND GUM BENZOIN
2 TEASPOONS CINNAMON POWDER
1 TEASPOON CLOVES
1 STAR ANISE
PEEL OF AN ORANGE
4 DROPS ROSE OIL
2 DROPS LAVENDER OIL
WHOLE ROSES TO DECORATE

*The **Small Bowl** (p.58) is filled with this
dry rose pot pourri, a traditional mix.*

BLUE & WHITE MIX

500ml (1pt) KESU FLOWERS
500ml (1pt) MIXED PALE BLUE
& WHITE FLOWERS
60g (2oz) ROSEMARY
30g (1oz) LAVENDER
30g (1oz) ORRIS ROOT POWDER
2 TEASPOONS CINNAMON POWDER
1/2 TEASPOON CORIANDER SEEDS
4 DROPS BOIS DE ROSE OIL
2 DROPS GERANIUM OIL
WHITE SEA CARROT,
BLUE COLUMBINES
& BLUE AZALEAS TO DECORATE

*The **Blue Platter** (p.59) is decorated with
this elegant blue and white dry pot pourri.*

TRADITIONAL ROSE MIX

500ml (1pt) MIXED WHOLE ROSES
& ROSE PETALS
500ml (1pt) MIXED CALAMUS
& WOODRUFF LEAVES
30g (1oz) ORRIS ROOT POWDER
4 CRUSHED TONQUIN BEANS
2 CHOPPED VANILLA PODS
2 TEASPOONS ALLSPICE
2 TEASPOONS CRUSHED AMBRETTE SEEDS
2 TEASPOONS CRUSHED MACE
4 DROPS CLARY SAGE OIL
4 DROPS ROSE OIL
2 DROPS BERGAMOT OIL
WHOLE ROSES TO DECORATE

*The large middle compartment of the
Three-dimensional Fan (pp.66-7) is
filled with this musky dry pot pourri.*

POT POURRIS FOR SACHETS

HELIOTROPE MIX

1 litre (2pt) HELIOTROPE FLOWERS
OR ROSE PETALS
60g (2oz) ORRIS ROOT POWDER
4 GROUND TONQUIN BEANS
2 CHOPPED VANILLA PODS
6 DROPS HELIOTROPE OIL

*The **Flower Garden Sachet** (p.65) is
filled with this sweet-scented dry pot pourri.
Try using 4 drops of rose oil, 4 drops of
neroli oil, 2 chopped vanilla pods
and 2 drops of almond essence
instead of the heliotrope oil.*

ROSE, PATCHOULI & GERANIUM MIX

500ml (1pt) SCENTED GERANIUM
(PELARGONIUM) LEAVES
500ml (1pt) DRY, FRAGRANT SAWDUST
60g (2oz) LAVENDER
30g (1oz) ORRIS ROOT POWDER
1 TEASPOON CLOVES
4 DROPS GERANIUM OIL
4 DROPS ROSE OIL
2 DROPS PATCHOULI OIL

*The **Chair Sachets** (p.64) are filled
with this rich, evocative dry pot pourri.*

❀ CANDLE *Tiny
scented candles
are delightful in
the dining room.*

TRADITIONAL ROSE-PETAL MOIST MIX

1 litre (2pt) CRUMBLED
STOCK-POT PETALS
60g (2oz) LAVENDER
60g (2oz) CHOPPED ANGELICA
AND/OR ERYNGIUM ROOT
30g (1oz) ORRIS ROOT POWDER
PEEL OF 1/2 AN ORANGE
1 TEASPOON CLOVES
4 DROPS ROSE OIL
2 DROPS LAVENDER OIL
2 DROPS GERANIUM,
SPIKENARD OR SUMBUL OIL

*The **Silk Hearts** (p.65) are filled
with this rosy moist pot pourri.*

BERGAMOT MIX

500ml (1pt) BERGAMOT LEAVES
& FLOWERS
500ml (1pt) MIXED CALAMUS,
MELILOT AND/
OR SWEET VERNAL
GRASS & WOODRUFF
30g (1oz) LAVENDER
30g (1oz) ORRIS ROOT POWDER
2 TONQUIN BEANS
1 TEASPOON ALLSPICE
4 DROPS MONARDA OIL
2 DROPS ANGELICA OIL
2 DROPS GERANIUM OIL

*The **Regency Elegance Sachets**
(p.65) are filled with this sharp,
musky dry pot pourri.*

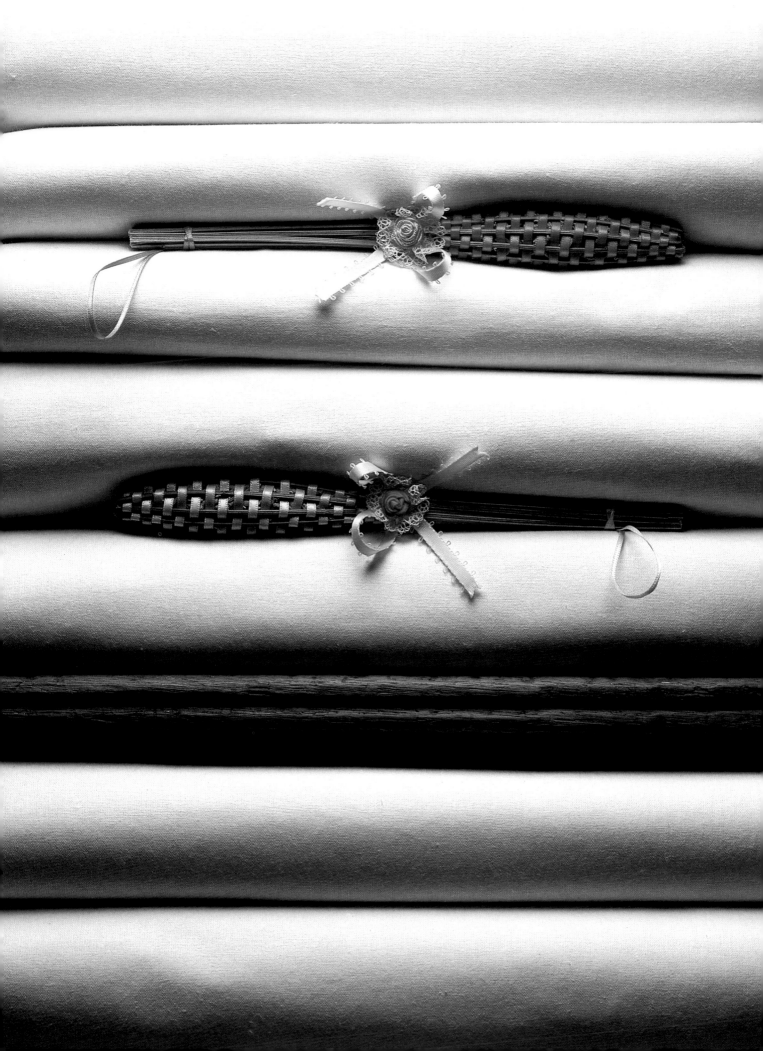

THE BEDROOM

WHATEVER THE STYLE of your bedroom – intimate and Victorian, stark and modern, or traditional and chintzy – you can make it redolent with complementary perfumes. An ideal pot pourri for the bedroom is the lovely rose, lavender and carnation mix, which you can sharpen by adding peppermint, orange or lemon. Fill pillows with soothing pot pourris. Try stuffing a large pillow with a hop, lemon and lavender mix – recommended by George III as an excellent sleep inducer. Another traditional filler for pillows is a mixture of woodruff and agrimony leaves. The coumarin contained in them becomes more fragrant with age. Old, white lacy pillows, cushions and nightdress cases, beloved of the Victorians, look delightful in almost any bedroom, as do little antique lace sachets, although you can use any fabric

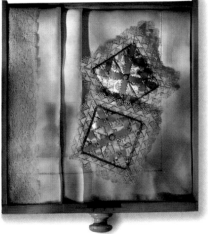

❀ SCENTED DELIGHTS *The exquisite lavender bundles (left) and the delicate sachets (above) are ideal for scenting clothes and linen.*

you like. Fill sachets with much stronger mixes than pillows. Make these soft and floral, hot and spicy, herby or even camphorous. Pop little moth repellant sachets in drawers and hang them in wardrobes. Drawer liners can also be scented with a moth repellant mix, or you can try a floral one if you prefer. Floral pomanders are lovely and a little unusual, or try making simple citrus pomanders – men often prefer the hot fragrance. Unglazed lidded pots will diffuse perfume into the room. Just drop a little essential oil into the pot before filling it

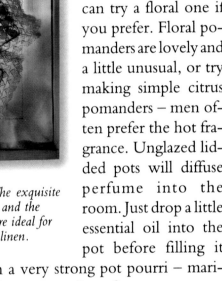

with a very strong pot pourri – marigold is an excellent fragrance to use. Place the pots by the bedside so that the soothing perfume drifts over you as you sleep. Store natural beauty products in old bottles or jars. Arranged on the dressing table they are both useful and decorative.

❀ NIGHTDRESS CASE
(below) Place a scented
sachet, filled with a
favourite mix, in your
nightdress case.

❀ SCATTER CUSHIONS
Scented with a gentle and
soothing pot pourri, these
lovely lacy pillows (above
and below) produce a
beautiful subtle fragrance
and are an attractive
decoration for the bedroom.

❧ SATIN & WHITE LACE ❧

PILLOWS FOR THE BEDROOM can be
filled with soothing herbal mixes
or light, floral pot pourris. Arranged
on the bed, they will perfume the
whole room as well as scenting the
bedlinen. Try filling the pillows
with a mix containing hops –
traditionally held to be a relaxant
– and the gentle fragrance will
help you to sleep. White pillow
cases embroidered or covered
with lace look lovely in any
bedroom as their traditional
designs complement most
decorations. If you prefer
to have patterned pillow-
cases, use muted colours
to complement
relaxing fragrances,
and bright colours
to accentuate
more pervasive
perfumes.

❀ SLEEP PILLOW
*Filled with a soothing
mix, largely of hops
but with a hint of
lavender, this pillow
is beneficial for all
those who have
trouble sleeping.*

❧ POMANDERS & SACHETS ❧

SCENTED DECORATIONS that can be suspended are useful for the bedroom where flat surfaces may be limited to the bedside table and the dressing table. Hang floral pomanders in eye-catching positions – from the curtain rail perhaps, or over the dressing-table mirror. Place citrus pomanders in similar positions or hang them in the wardrobe where they will transfer their tangy scent to your clothes. Pretty cloth sachets are perfect for looping over door handles, drawer knobs, radiators or any suitable hook. Pastel shades are very often best for the bedroom. However, a wonderful way to make a stunning impact in a simply decorated bedroom is to create sachets and pomanders in bold colours.

✿ CITRUS & LACE *A tangy, orange pomander surrounded by lacy netting can be put on show in the bedroom.*

✿ BLUE & WHITE HEARTS *Hang this elegant, camphor- and lavender-scented sachet chain in front of a window or beside the dressing table for a lovely effect.*

✿ RIBBON SACHETS *These two scented sachets match the floral pomanders opposite in both fragrance and appearance. They are lovely grouped together.*

❀ RIBBON & LACE
This beautiful sachet is filled with a mixed floral pot pourri and would look beautiful hanging in front of dark curtains or furniture.

❀ LAVENDER-BLUE POMANDER *Made from lavender flowers and blue floral ribbon, this pomander is scented with lavender and cloves.*

❀ ROSE-RED POMANDER
Decorated with a variety of bright pink and red flowers, this pretty rose-scented, floral pomander is truly eye-catching.

❧ CREAMS, FLORAL WATERS & COLOGNES ❧

PERFUMES AND COSMETICS are simple to make at home and, as well as being natural, they are a wonderful addition to the scent and decoration of the bedroom. Flowers, herbs and essential oils are used to perfume home-made cosmetics. The scent you choose is a matter of personal preference, although some plants, such as elderflowers and chamomile, are particularly suitable for making creams and oils as they possess soothing and cleansing properties. Choose attractive bottles, jars and pots for your perfumes and cosmetics, and decorate them with ribbons and pressed flowers.

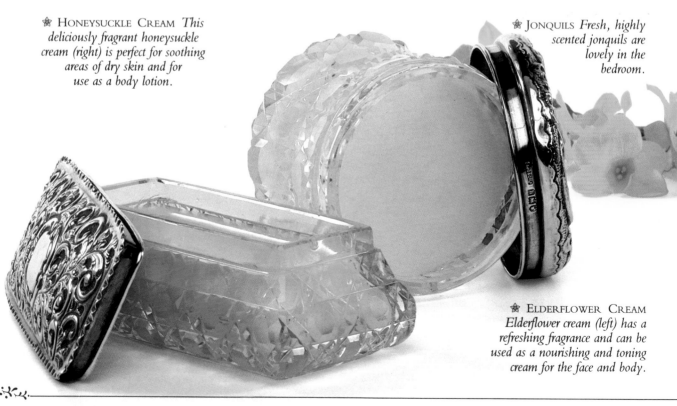

❀ HONEYSUCKLE CREAM *This deliciously fragrant honeysuckle cream (right) is perfect for soothing areas of dry skin and for use as a body lotion.*

❀ JONQUILS *Fresh, highly scented jonquils are lovely in the bedroom.*

❀ ELDERFLOWER CREAM *Elderflower cream (left) has a refreshing fragrance and can be used as a nourishing and toning cream for the face and body.*

❀ FLORAL COLOGNES
*Sweet-scented flowers can
be used to produce lovely
colognes. These bottles (far
left) contain jonquil
cologne (see p.120)
and violet and
heliotrope cologne.*

❀ ROSE WATER & BODY OIL
*The dark blue bottle (far right)
contains rose water – a sweet-
scented perfume. Body oil
(right), made with almond
oil and any essential oil,
(see p.120) is perfect
for softening the skin.*

❀ FRAGRANT TALCUM POWDER
*A few drops of a favourite essential
oil transforms unscented talc
into something special.*

❀ HAND CREAM *This
hand cream is
scented with
a few drops
of essential oil.*

❧ POT POURRIS ❧

PRETTY AND DELICATE floral pot pourris are popular for the bedroom, as they lend themselves well to the soothing, pastel colours in which many bedrooms are decorated. However, if your bedroom is filled with primary colours and bold abstracts, then create a pot pourri that is as vibrant as its surroundings. A formally decorated pot pourri looks wonderful in a bedroom full of stripes and geometric shapes, while informal designs are more suited to a floral décor. Display the pot pourri on the dressing table or make matching mixes for each bedside table. Do not make the scent so strong that your sleep is disturbed and, if you have made herb pillows for the bed, ensure that the perfume of your mix complements that of the pillows.

STATICE

ROSE

POTENTILLA

LAVENDER

GLOBE AMARANTH

❀ SHALLOW DISH
The pattern of this vibrant pink pot pourri (above) is just like a formal flower border. The musky carnation scent is lifted by tangy orange.

ROSES

ANAPHALIS
(DYED PINK)

BLUEBELLS

❀ NAUTILUS SHELL
*The moist pot pourri inside
this polished nautilus shell
is decorated with rose buds
and bluebells, so that its
soothing, traditional scent
of rose and lavender
escapes slowly.*

ROSE BUDS

ROSES

KESU

DEUTZIA

POTENTILLA

BLUEBELLS

POLYGONUM
CAMPANULATUM

❀ SMALL SILVER
BOWL *Peppermint oil
gently sharpens the
overall floral perfume
of this dark blue pot
pourri (right), which
is decorated with
roses, deutzia
blossoms and
bluebells.*

ROSES

❧ CERAMIC STYLES ❧

SMALL, SELF-CONTAINED SCENTED DECORATIONS are ideal for the bedroom, especially if space is limited. Ornamental, unglazed ceramic pots make excellent containers for pot pourris or essential oils. The scent of the mixture is absorbed by the unglazed pottery and exudes slowly into the room, allowing the use of a strong perfume that might otherwise be too overpowering for the bedroom. Decorative, unglazed ceramic shapes, such as the hearts below, are useful for placing in odd corners, for scenting jewellery boxes, wardrobes and chests of drawers, and for making a display on the dressing table or the bedside table. Perfume the shapes by soaking them in a fragrant essence or essential oil. Other small and attractive items, such as shells, are also suitable for displaying in the bedroom and are easily scented in the same way, or by putting a few drops of an essential oil or pot-pourri reviver in their centres. If you enjoy strong, heady perfumes, try burning one or two joss sticks. Make sure that you like the perfume before you light them as the scent tends to be very persistent.

❀ LARGE DECORATIVE TERRACOTTA JAR *This attractive blue, red and white jar is filled with a richly fragrant, mixed-flower pot pourri that complements its colours.*

❀ BLUE HEARTS *Several, small pottery hearts, scented with lavender essence or an essential oil, make a simple decoration.*

✿ MATCHING
TERRACOTTA JARS
*Filled with a lightly
scented rose, lavender
and peppermint pot
pourri, these jars are
ideal for displaying
on the bedside table.*

✿ SHELLS *The shapes
of seashells make them
naturally decorative.
They are scented
with a rose
perfume.*

STAR TURBAN

TURBAN SHELL

STRIPED TOP

✿ JOSS STICKS
*These simple room
perfumers from the
East can be used to
create a mysterious,
hazy atmosphere in
the bedroom.*

COMMERCIAL TROCHUS

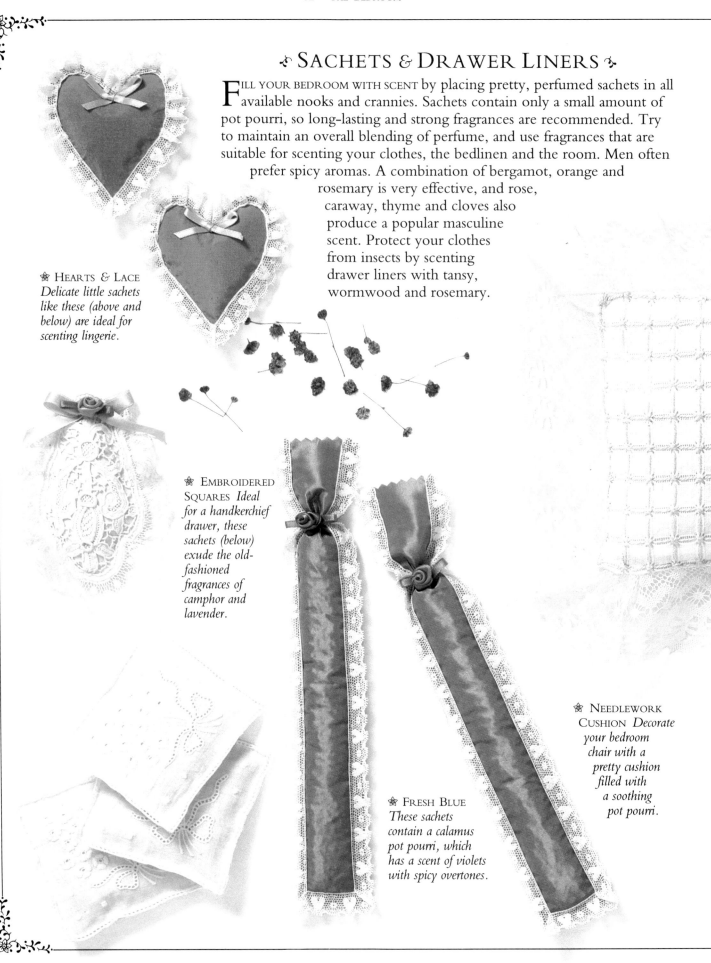

❧ SACHETS & DRAWER LINERS ❧

FILL YOUR BEDROOM WITH SCENT by placing pretty, perfumed sachets in all available nooks and crannies. Sachets contain only a small amount of pot pourri, so long-lasting and strong fragrances are recommended. Try to maintain an overall blending of perfume, and use fragrances that are suitable for scenting your clothes, the bedlinen and the room. Men often prefer spicy aromas. A combination of bergamot, orange and rosemary is very effective, and rose, caraway, thyme and cloves also produce a popular masculine scent. Protect your clothes from insects by scenting drawer liners with tansy, wormwood and rosemary.

❀ HEARTS & LACE
Delicate little sachets like these (above and below) are ideal for scenting lingerie.

❀ EMBROIDERED SQUARES *Ideal for a handkerchief drawer, these sachets (below) exude the old-fashioned fragrances of camphor and lavender.*

❀ NEEDLEWORK CUSHION *Decorate your bedroom chair with a pretty cushion filled with a soothing pot pourri.*

❀ FRESH BLUE
These sachets contain a calamus pot pourri, which has a scent of violets with spicy overtones.

❀ DRAWER LINERS
*Line your drawers
with perfumed paper
to ensure that your
clothes are always
sweetly scented.*

❀ DAINTY LACE
*Round or square,
lace sachets are
perfect for placing
among clothes
and bedlinen.*

❧ RECIPES ❧

FOR THE BODY

ROSE WATER

250ml (½pt) VODKA
10 DROPS ROSE OIL

Rose Water (p.77). Add rose oil to vodka. Shake well. Bottle and cork.

VIOLET & HELIOTROPE COLOGNE

120g (4oz) ORRIS ROOT
250ml (½pt) VODKA
4 DROPS HELIOTROPE OIL

Violet & Heliotrope Cologne (p.77). Put orris root and vodka in a jar. Infuse for 10 days, shaking daily. Strain and add heliotrope oil. Shake well. Bottle and cork.

ELDERFLOWER CREAM

180ml (6fl oz) ALMOND OIL
1 TABLESPOON LANOLIN
1 CUP ELDERFLOWERS

Elderflower Cream (p.76). Melt lanolin in a bowl placed in a pan of hot water. Mix in almond oil. Add elderflowers. Heat in a pan of simmering water for 30 minutes. Strain and cool. Pack in a lidded jar.

HONEYSUCKLE CREAM

120g (4oz) PETROLEUM JELLY
30g (1oz) FRESH HONEYSUCKLE BLOSSOM
3 DROPS HONEYSUCKLE OIL

Honeysuckle Cream (p.76). Melt petroleum jelly in a bowl placed in a pan of hot water. Add blossom. Heat mixture in a pan of simmering water for 30 minutes. Strain, add essential oil and cool. Pack in a lidded jar.

POT POURRIS FOR SACHETS

CALAMUS MIX

500g (1pt) CALAMUS LEAVES
500g (1pt) ROSE-SCENTED GERANIUM (PELARGONIUM) LEAVES
30g (1oz) LAVENDER
30g (1oz) ORRIS ROOT POWDER
GRATED RIND OF AN ORANGE
1 TEASPOON CINNAMON POWDER
4 DROPS GERANIUM OIL
2 DROPS ORANGE OIL
2 DROPS ROSE OIL

*The **Fresh Blue Sachets** (p.82) and the **Lace Sachets** (p.83) contain this spicy dry pot pourri.*

LAVENDER MIX

1 litre (2pt) LAVENDER
30g (1oz) ORRIS ROOT POWDER
2 TEASPOONS CLOVES
6 DROPS LAVENDER OIL
2 DROPS CLOVE OIL

*The **Blue-flowered Ribbon Sachet** (p.74) is filled with this pleasing dry pot pourri, which complements that of the **Lavender-blue Pomander** (p.75).*

ROSE MIX

1 litre (2pt) ROSE PETALS
30g (1oz) ORRIS ROOT POWDER
6 DROPS ROSE OIL
2 DROPS CLARY SAGE OIL

*The **Pink-flowered Ribbon Sachet** (p.74) is filled with a dry pot pourri that is rose-scented with a hint of musk, a perfect match to the **Rose-red Pomander** (p.75).*

CARMELITE MIX

500ml (1pt) ORANGE FLOWERS
500ml (1pt) LEMON BALM
60g (2oz) CHOPPED ANGELICA ROOT
30g (1oz) ORRIS ROOT POWDER
PEEL OF 2 LEMONS
1 GRATED NUTMEG
2 TEASPOONS CLOVES
2 TEASPOONS CORIANDER SEEDS
1 TEASPOON CINNAMON POWDER
4 DROPS NEROLI OIL
2 DROPS CORIANDER OIL
2 DROPS LEMON OIL

*The **Nightdress Case** (p.72), the **Ribbon & Lace Sachet** (p.75) and the **Needlework Cushion** (pp.82-3) are all scented with this soothing dry pot pourri.*

MOTH-REPELLENT MIX

60g (2oz) ROSEMARY
60g (2oz) TANSY
60g (2oz) WORMWOOD
30g (1oz) ORRIS ROOT POWDER
1 CRUSHED CINNAMON STICK
2 TEASPOONS CLOVES
4 DROPS ROSEMARY OIL

*The **Drawer Liners** (p.83) are scented with this dry pot pourri, which is also suitable for filling small sachets.*

CAMPHOR & LAVENDER MIX

120g (4oz) LAVENDER
60g (2oz) MINT
30g (1oz) FINE-GROUND GUM BENZOIN
1 TEASPOON CLOVES
1 TEASPOON CORIANDER SEEDS
1 CRUMBLED STAR ANISE
3 DROPS CAMPHOR OIL
3 DROPS LAVENDER OIL

*The **Embroidered Squares** and the **Hearts & Lace Sachets** (p.82) are filled with this dry pot pourri, which has a wonderful piercing scent. The **Blue & White Hearts** (p.74) also contain this basic mix but larkspur flowers are used in place of the mint, which makes the fragrance slightly less sharp.*

POT POURRIS FOR PILLOWS & CUSHIONS

SLEEP MIX

750ml (1½pt) HOPS
250ml (½pt) LEMON BALM
60g (2oz) LAVENDER
30g (1oz) ORRIS ROOT POWDER
1 TEASPOON CLOVES
1 TEASPOON CRUSHED CARDAMOM SEEDS
2 DROPS CLOVE OIL
2 DROPS LAVENDER OIL
2 DROPS MELISSA (LEMON BALM) OIL

The **Scatter Cushions** and **Sleep Pillow** (pp.72-3) are filled with this dry pot pourri.

POT POURRIS FOR CONTAINERS

FLORAL MIX

500ml (1pt) MIXED GARDEN FLOWERS
500ml (1pt) BAY LEAVES & MYRTLE
60g (2oz) LAVENDER
30g (1oz) ORRIS ROOT POWDER
1 BROKEN CINNAMON STICK
2 TEASPOONS CLOVES
2 DROPS CARNATION OIL
2 DROPS LEMON OIL
2 DROPS ROSE OIL

The **Large Terracotta Jar** (p.80) contains this dry mix. The **Matching Terracotta Jars** (p.81) are also filled with the same basic mix but with roses and peppermint as the main ingredients.

POT POURRIS FOR DISPLAY

MUSKY MIX

1 litre (2pt) MIXED PINK FLOWERS
60g (2oz) LAVENDER
30g (1oz) ORRIS ROOT POWDER
2 TEASPOONS CINNAMON POWDER
3 CRUSHED TONQUIN BEANS
1 CHOPPED VANILLA POD
PEEL OF AN ORANGE
4 DROPS CARNATION OIL
2 DROPS ORANGE OIL

The **Shallow Dish** (p.78) displays this musky but sharp dry pot pourri.

❀ FLOWER RIBBON SACHETS *These sachets are ideal in the wardrobe or on display.*

LUXURIOUS MIX

1 litre (2pt) STOCK-POT PETALS
30g (1oz) LAVENDER
30g (1oz) ORRIS ROOT POWDER
2 TEASPOONS CINNAMON POWDER
½ CHOPPED VANILLA POD
½ TEASPOON CRUSHED CLOVES
4 DROPS ROSE OIL
2 DROPS LAVENDER OIL
ROSE BUDS & BLUEBELLS TO DECORATE

The **Nautilus Shell** (p.79) is filled with this rose- and lavender-scented moist pot pourri, which is ideal for the bedroom.

FLOWER & HERB MIX

500ml (1pt) ROSES & ROSE PETALS
500ml (1pt) KESU FLOWERS
60g (2oz) MIXED SWEET HERBS
30g (1oz) ORRIS ROOT POWDER
½ TEASPOON CRUSHED CARDAMOM SEEDS
4 DROPS ANY FLORAL OIL
2 DROPS PEPPERMINT OIL

The **Small Silver Bowl** (p.79) displays this mainly floral dry pot pourri.

THE NURSERY

❋

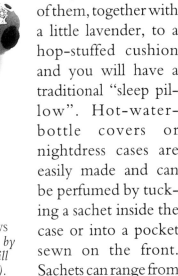

THERE IS NO BETTER WAY to encourage a love of the natural world in your child than by taking him or her into the garden to gather herbs and flowers that will ultimately be used to fill toys. Your child will remember plant names and fragrances with enthusiasm, and will love to be in- volved in making the toys. There are many playthings you can make that can also be scented. Simply adapt any ideas you have to include either a pot pourri stuffing or a scented sachet. For example, dolls full of lavender, herb-stuffed teddies and a curious Suffolk puff caterpil- lar, which is made of patchwork circles each filled with a different mix. Noth- ing could be more exciting to a child than an array of fragrances. In the nine- teenth century it was recommended that nurseries were scented with the spicy aromas of cloves, nutmeg, cinnamon and caraway. How- ever, children soon discover their own favourite scents. These often relate to the familiar smell of the kitchen – orange and lemon, and peppermint and spearmint are all popular. These fresh aromas are ideal for the nursery because they are also quite soothing; add one or two of them, together with a little lavender, to a hop-stuffed cushion and you will have a traditional "sleep pil- low". Hot-water- bottle covers or nightdress cases are easily made and can be perfumed by tuck- ing a sachet inside the case or into a pocket sewn on the front. Sachets can range from rose-scented dolls to tiny lavender teddies and from little herby chicks to simple spicy squares. Bright colours are beloved of children and look delightful in the nursery. Of course, there are some children who prefer subdued colours and more sophisticated perfumes. So work with them when scenting and decorating their rooms.

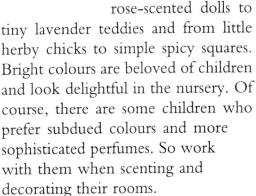

❋ FRAGRANT TOYS & PILLOWS
Brighten and perfume the nursery by making scented toys (above) or fill pillows with fragrant mixes (left).

❋

❋❋ NOT ALL THE TOYS SHOWN
HERE ARE SUITABLE FOR PLAYING
WITH, AND CARE SHOULD BE TAKEN
TO DISPLAY THEM OUT OF THE
REACH OF VERY YOUNG CHILDREN.

❋ GREEN TEDDY *Made
from nylon lace and filled
with a lemon-scented mix,
this teddy is only suitable
for decorative purposes.*

❋ SLEEP TEDDY
*This teddy is filled
with a soothing
peppermint and hop
mixture. Hang him out of
reach over the bed or cot.*

❋ TEDDIES & CHICKS
*Made to match the
bigger toys, these
herb-scented
sachets can be
tucked between
clothes or bedlinen.*

❋ MOTHER HEN *Filled
with a herby mix, this
colourful hen looks lovely
when displayed with
her two yellow chicks.*

❧ AROMATIC TOYS ❧

A ROMATIC SOFT TOYS add a new dimension to the nursery. Hang a lavender doll in the nursery and the scent of lavender will fill the room. Teddy and chicken sachets are simple to make and they, too, will gently perfume the air; alternatively, tucked into drawers they will sweeten the contents. If you are making toys for very young children, encase the pot pourri in fire-resistant wadding to make them safe to play with, or display them out of reach.

❀ FLORAL DOLLS *Easily made from tiny scraps of material and filled with rose petals, these sachet dolls are perfect for putting in chests of drawers and cupboards.*

❀ DAINTY DOLLS *Embroidered faces, lace and ribbons transform these simple sachets into lovely dolls.*

❀ LAVENDER LILY *This enchanting doll is made with net material and filled with lavender. She is the ideal decoration for a little girl's nursery and will imbue the room with the fragrance of lavender.*

Traditional Crafts

Patchwork and wickerwork are among the many crafts that can provide inspiration for scented decorations in the nursery. The long tradition of these crafts ensures that most of the items you choose will blend in with almost any nursery. Sew your patchwork using cloth of bright, primary colours and all children will be captivated. Plain wickerwork can be painted and varnished to make it more attractive. Children generally like lemon, rose, lavender and herbal scents – peppermint in particular is very popular – so it is best to make most of your mixtures in this scent range unless your child has a special preference.

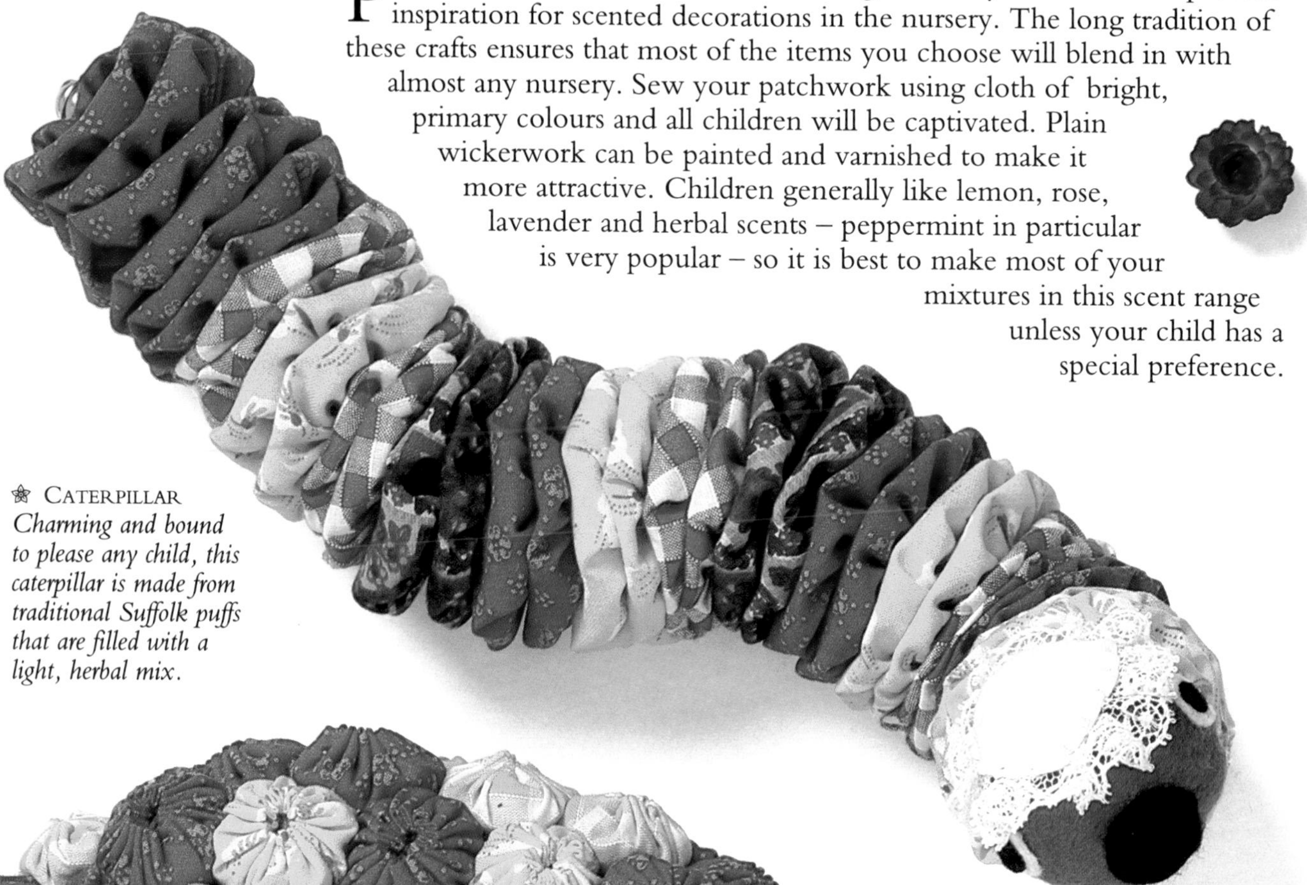

Caterpillar *Charming and bound to please any child, this caterpillar is made from traditional Suffolk puffs that are filled with a light, herbal mix.*

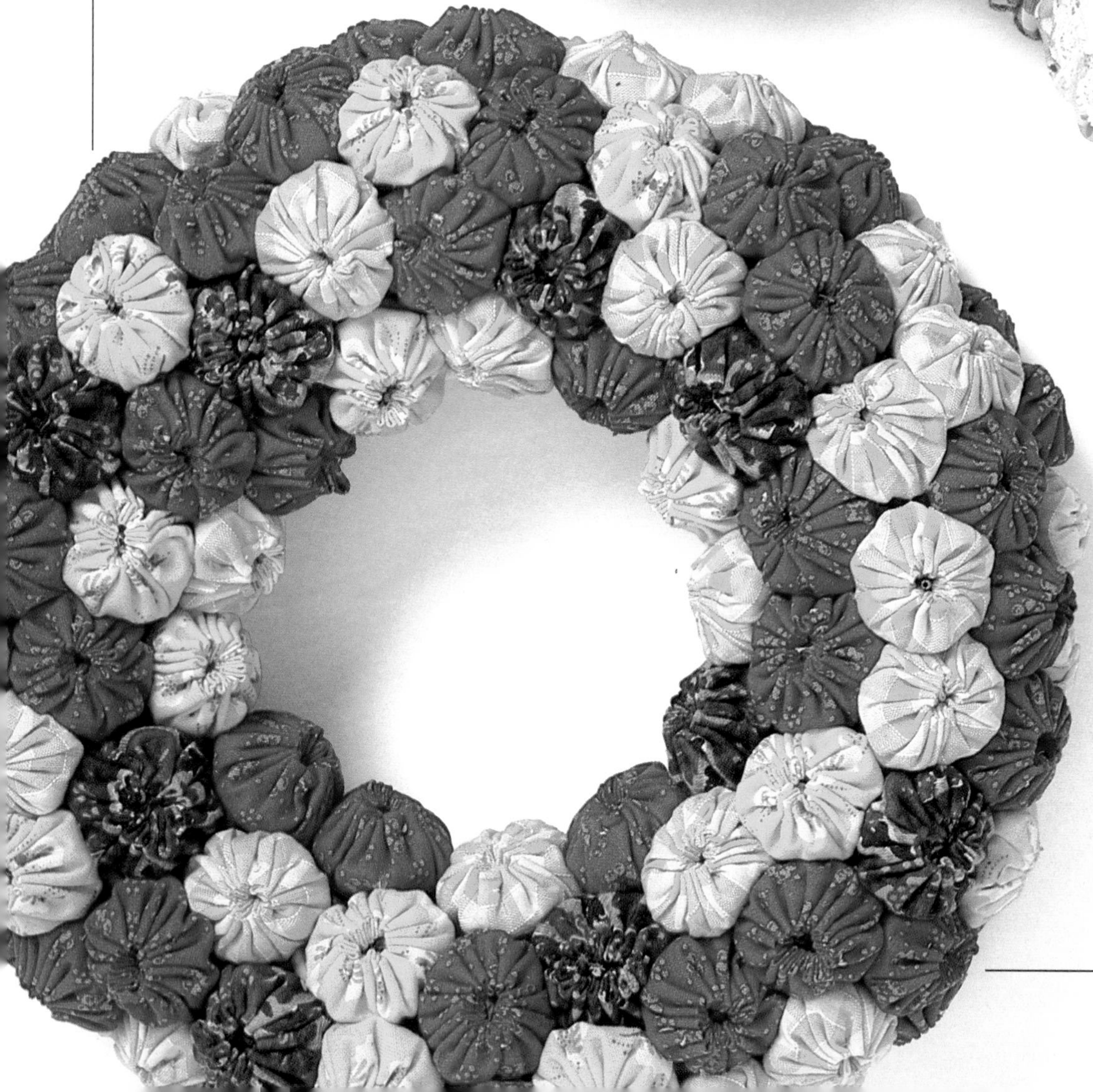

Nursery Garland *Tightly stuffed Suffolk puffs are glued on top of a wickerwork base to produce this lovely, brightly coloured and strongly scented garland, which is ideal for displaying on a shelf or hanging on the nursery wall.*

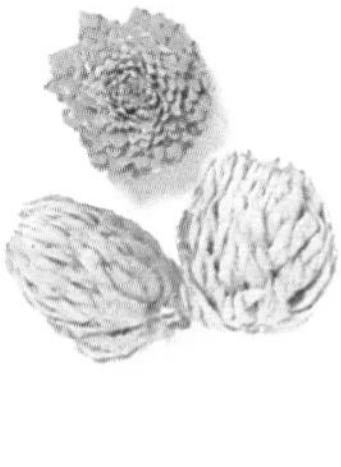

❀ CANEWORK
CHICKEN *This
chicken is ideal for
a nursery as children
cannot spill the pot
pourri but the lemon
scent will easily filter
through the cane.*

❀ PATCHWORK
SACHETS *Sachets,
lightly filled with
a rose and lavender
pot pourri or a delicate
herbal mixture, are ideal
for tucking into drawers
and the pockets of clothes
to keep them sweetly scented.*

❀ HOT-WATER-BOTTLE
COVER *A simple and useful
bedtime accessory, this hot-
water-bottle cover is scented
with sachets placed in
the little front pocket.*

❀ TEDDIES
*These sachets are
ideal for providing
a gentle perfume.
Fill each teddy
with a different
mix to vary
the fragrance
as desired.*

❀ GINGHAM
PYJAMA CASE *A
lovely pyjama case
brightens the cot
during the day
and scents the
nightwear kept
inside it.*

❧ TIME FOR BED ❧

Most children like to be tucked up with a teddy or doll or a comforter of some kind at bedtime. It is often a very simple object that reassures children who are afraid of the dark if they wake in the night. Regular bedtime accessories, such as hot-water-bottle covers, pillows and pyjama cases, are ideal companions, and are easily scented with sachets or by putting pot pourri inside an envelope of stuffing, which is then placed inside the cloth cover.

❀ CO-ORDINATING ACCESSORIES *Made with matching material and filled with complementary pot pourris, this pillow and pyjama case are wonderful additions to the nursery.*

❀ STRAW TOYS *Little straw toys are scented by being placed in a pot pourri or by rubbing them with a little essential oil.*

❧ RECIPES ❧

POT POURRIS FOR TOYS & DECORATIONS

FRESH MIX
---

1 litre (2pt) MIXED SWEET HERBS
60g (2oz) LAVENDER
30g (1oz) ORRIS ROOT POWDER
2 TEASPOONS CARAWAY SEEDS
2 TEASPOONS CRUSHED
CARDAMOM SEEDS
4 DROPS CLARY SAGE OIL
2 DROPS LAVENDER OIL

*The **Mother Hen** (p.88) is stuffed with this herbal dry pot pourri, which will freshen the air in the nursery.*

RED & YELLOW MIX

500ml (1pt) YELLOW
EVERLASTING FLOWERS
500ml (1pt) RED COCKSCOMB FLOWERS
60g (2oz) ROSEMARY
30g (1oz) FINE-GROUND GUM BENZOIN
2 TEASPOONS CRUSHED ALLSPICE BERRIES
1 BROKEN CINNAMON STICK
6 DROPS LEMON OIL
2 DROPS ROSEMARY OIL

*The **Canework Chicken** (p.91) is filled with this dry pot pourri. This brightly-coloured dry pot pourri can be displayed out of reach in the nursery or placed in a child-proof container.*

CHAMOMILE & LEMON MIX

500ml (1pt) CHAMOMILE FLOWERS
500ml (1pt) LEMON VERBENA
60g (2oz) ROSEMARY
30g (1oz) ORRIS ROOT POWDER
2 TEASPOONS CLOVES
1 TEASPOON CINNAMON POWDER
4 DROPS LEMON OIL
2 DROPS CHAMOMILE OIL
2 DROPS ROSEMARY OIL

*The **Green Teddy** (p.88) is filled with this dry pot pourri. It is lemon-scented with herby chamomile overtones.*

NURSERY SLEEP MIX

500ml (1pt) MIXED
MEADOWSWEET, MINTS
& ROSEMARY
500ml (1pt) HOPS
60g (2oz) LAVENDER
30g (1oz) ORRIS
ROOT POWDER
2 DROPS LAVENDER OIL
2 DROPS ROSEMARY OIL
2 DROPS PEPPERMINT OIL

*The **Sleep Teddy** (p.88) is filled with this delicious and soothing dry pot pourri, which will fill the nursery with a relaxing fragrance.*

POT POURRIS FOR CUSHIONS & CASES

ROSE & PINE MIX

500ml (1pt) ROSE PETALS
500ml (1pt) MIXED CONIFER TIPS
& PINE NEEDLES
60g (2oz) LAVENDER
30g (1oz) ORRIS
ROOT POWDER
2 TEASPOONS
ALLSPICE BERRIES
3 DROPS ROSE OIL
2 DROPS LAVENDER OIL
2 DROPS PINE OIL

*The **Gingham Pyjama Case** (p.92) is scented with this dry pot pourri. The rose petals make the mix sweet while the pine needles give it crisp overtones, producing a delicious scent.*

HOPS & MINT SLEEP MIX

500ml (1pt) HOPS
500ml (1pt) MIXED ALECOST & MINT
60g (2oz) LAVENDER
30g (1oz) ORRIS ROOT POWDER
GRATED RIND OF A LEMON
1 TEASPOON CRUSHED
CARDAMOM SEEDS
2 DROPS LEMON OIL
2 DROPS PEPPERMINT OIL
2 DROPS LAVENDER OIL

*The **Co-ordinating Accessories** (p.93) are scented with this dry pot pourri. It is a soothing sleep mix, wonderful for scenting pyjamas and nighties.*

POT POURRIS FOR SACHETS

ROSEMARY, THYME & CARAWAY MIX

500ml (1pt) ROSEMARY
500ml (1pt) THYME
2 TEASPOONS CARAWAY SEEDS
30g (1oz) ORRIS ROOT POWDER
3 DROPS ROSEMARY OIL
3 DROPS THYME OIL

❋ TEDDY SACHET
Teddy sachets can be filled with any mix and are always charming.

BASIC SPICE MIX

30g (1oz) CRUSHED CLOVES
30g (1oz) CARAWAY SEEDS
30g (1oz) CRUSHED CARDAMOM SEEDS
30g (1oz) CRUSHED ALLSPICE BERRIES
30g (1oz) ORRIS ROOT POWDER
4 DROPS CLOVE OIL
2 DROPS LAVENDER OIL

ROSEMARY MIX

1 litre (2pt) ROSEMARY
30g (1oz) ORRIS ROOT POWDER
4 DROPS ROSEMARY OIL

❀ NURSERY
GARLAND
*This Suffolk
puff garland
is lovely in the
nursery and is popular
with young children.*

MARJORAM & LEMON THYME MIX

1 litre (2pt) MIXED LEMON THYME
& MARJORAM
30g (1oz) ORRIS ROOT POWDER
4 DROPS LEMON OIL
2 DROPS MARJORAM OIL

LEMON VERBENA MIX

1 litre (2pt) LEMON VERBENA
30g (1oz) ORRIS ROOT POWDER
6 DROPS LEMON OIL

SIMPLE LAVENDER MIX

1 litre (2pt) LAVENDER
30g (1oz) ORRIS ROOT POWDER
6 DROPS LAVENDER OIL

*The assorted sachets on pp.88-93 are
filled with these pot pourris. They
are unsophisticated but lovely
and are all ideal for filling small
sachets that are to be placed
in hot-water-bottle covers and
in drawers and cupboards.
Each recipe makes enough
pot pourri for 8 sachets.*

SUFFOLK PUFFS

*Suffolk puffs are a traditional
patchwork design. Cut out a circle
of cloth and make a small hem all
around the edge using fairly large
stitches. Fill the centre of the circle with
the mix you desire, then gather the
thread, tie the ends and tuck them into
the centre of the puff. Continue
making puffs in this way until you have
enough for your design. The puff can
either be stuffed tightly or loosely
depending on the desired
effect. Suffolk puffs are
very easy to make
and children will
love to help.*

SUFFOLK PUFF CATERPILLAR

***Caterpillar** (p.90). Lightly fill
Suffolk puffs with dried herbs, flatten
them and sew them together
through their centres.*

GERANIUM & LAVENDER MIX

500ml (1pt) GROUND IVY LEAVES
500ml (1pt) SCENTED GERANIUM
(PELARGONIUM) LEAVES
60g (2oz) LAVENDER
30g (1oz) ORRIS ROOT POWDER
2 TEASPOONS CINNAMON
POWDER
2 TEASPOONS GROUND CLOVES
4 DROPS GERANIUM OIL
2 DROPS LAVENDER OIL
2 DROPS YLANG YLANG OIL

*The **Nursery Garland** (p.90) is filled
with this dry pot pourri. This strongly
scented mix is popular among children.*

THE BATHROOM

BEAUTIFUL, perfumed pot pourris, pretty bouquets and garlands, baskets of flowers and stunning botanical friezes will transform any bathroom. Shells, sea glass, mosses, lichens, flowers, and silks and satins can all be found in wonderful shades of aquamarine, which, when they are mixed with mauve-blues, produce diffused, underwater colours that are ideal for the bathroom. Create contrasts by adding touches of pink and dark red, or yellow and orange to these hues. Large Abalone shells, with their wonderful, iridescent green linings, make beautiful containers for pot pourris. Decorated with whole flowers and spices they become pretty, textured tapestries. Try filling a large terracotta basket with dried flowers. Add artificially dyed flowers in shades of turquoise, jade and pink to accentuate the colours of the sea. Make substantial and opulent bouquets or tiny nosegays. Embellish garlands with small, scented shells and sea glass, fragrant flowers and even seaweed. Alternatively, adorn your wall with a luxuriant frieze – create a delicate landscape of pressed flowers, mosses and lichens. Use a floral sealer to protect dried-flower arrangements from the steamy atmosphere. Mix floral scents with sharp lemon, pine, geranium and orange to refresh their sweetness. Anise and orange makes an interesting combination, as does rose and orange. On the other hand, you may prefer the sweet oriental perfumes of ylang ylang or exquisite jasmine. Store home-made bath essences, oils, shampoos and toilet vinegars in antique bottles and decorate them with dried flowers and ribbons to add to the overall charm of the bathroom.

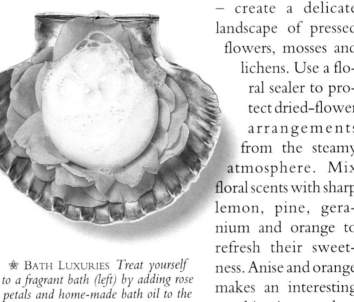

❀ BATH LUXURIES *Treat yourself to a fragrant bath (left) by adding rose petals and home-made bath oil to the water and using essential oil soap.*

❧ SACHETS & FRIEZE ❧

THERE ARE MANY different and effective ways of decorating the bathroom with scented displays. Hang sachets from the wall, over taps and from door and window handles. Fill the sachets with your favourite scents, complementing those of your soaps and shampoos. Pressed-flower collages are also effective. A frieze, such as the one below, adds individuality and colour to the bathroom and will lend the room a gentle perfume.

❀ SEA SACHETS
Filled with a floral mix, these sachets are made with strips of silk.

❀ SWINGING SCENT *Small, lemon-scented sachets, tied to a wooden ring, are ideal for hanging from the curtain rail.*

✾ BLUE BELLES
*A jasmine pot
pourri fills
these pretty
hanging
sachets.*

✾ RUBY SACHET
*A pressed-flower
decoration adds
the finishing touch
to this charming sachet.*

✾ FLORAL
SQUARES *Perfect
for display or for
scenting towels in the
linen cupboard, these
sachets are filled with
rosemary and southernwood.*

✾ FRIEZE *This
frieze is made by
arranging delicate pressed
flowers in a landscape of
mosses. The mosses are
scented with chamomile oil to
provide a long-lasting fragrance.*

❧ POSIES & WREATHS ❧

THE SEASIDE is a particularly apt and traditional theme to follow when decorating the bathroom. In your posies and wreaths use colours that are in keeping with the seaside – turquoise, blue and sea-green are ideal as they evoke clear skies and enticing water. Flowers that have been dyed blue or green will not look out of place, especially if used sparingly to highlight the appearance of the mix. Add shells and pebbles to the plant material, to complete the theme. All sorts of scents suit the bathroom and, although the fragrance you choose should not be overpowering, it can be quite strong. Hang posies and wreaths on walls, from the ceiling, on the side of the bath, or on the mirror.

ANAPHALIS (DYED JADE)

LAVENDER

❀ LARGE POSY *Among the medley of flowers used in this pretty bouquet are everlasting flowers and sea carrot. Rose oil, dropped in the centres of the rose buds, mingles with the perfume of the lavender.*

❀ PETITE POSY *This charming little posy, which matches the seaside wreath in colour, is scented with star anise and orange oil.*

❀ SEA GLASS *These pretty glass fragments were scented by steeping them in a jar of perfumed essence.*

ANAPHALIS
(DYED PINK)

ROSE

❀ SEASIDE WREATH *This
wreath is scented with lemon and
bergamot oils and is reminiscent
of the seaside in its display of
shells and colours such as sea-
green, cream and turquoise.*

❀ FORMAL CIRCLET
*The scent of roses and
geranium oil pervades
this circlet of red roses
and pink- and jade-
dyed anaphalis.*

SEA CARROT

STATICE

✿ BUBBLE BATHS
Floral or spicy perfumes can be used to make luxurious bubble baths.

❧ SOAPS & SHAMPOOS ❧

SPECIAL SOAPS and shampoos, bath oils, bubble baths and toilet vinegars are lovely to have in the bathroom. All these toiletries are simple to make at home and can be scented with your favourite fragrances. Decorate the bottles with dried flowers and pretty ribbons, and they will look lovely arranged on the shelves and around the bath.

❀ TOILET VINEGAR *Geranium leaves and oakmoss scent this toilet vinegar (far right).*

❀ HAIR RINSE *After shampooing, a chamomile hair rinse (centre) is perfect for reviving the hair.*

❀ BATH OIL *(right) This relaxing bath oil is scented with orange and rose essential oils.*

Rosa

❀ DRY SHAMPOO *Scented with rosemary, this dry shampoo (left) quickly refreshes your hair.*

❀ BATH BAGS *Filled with dried herbs, these sachets (above) will make your bath water scented and refreshing.*

❀ ESSENTIAL OIL SOAP *These soaps are lovely for guests or for your own personal use.*

❀ TERRACOTTA BASKET
*This terracotta basket is filled
with an assortment of dried plant
material, including larkspur,
dyed anaphalis and woodrush.
The arrangement is scented with
a sweet, tangy blend of Bois
de Rose oil and orange oil.*

❀ GLASS JAR *Layers of
lavender, larkspur, kesu flowers
and rose petals, decorated with
blue- and pink-dyed anaphalis,
fill this blue-green jar. Each layer
is scented with 4 drops of rose oil
and 4 drops of clary sage oil for
a rich and musky fragrance.*

ᕃ DESIGNS WITH DRIED FLOWERS ᕄ

Large arrangements of long-lasting dried flowers will transform a bathroom. Use your creative abilities to produce stunning displays – perhaps a basket brimming with pretty, chintzy flowers, or a formal porcelain container full of boldly coloured botanicals. Try using artificially dyed flowers: they are ideal for the bathroom as their bright colours will not fade in the steamy atmosphere. If you prefer more subtle colours make sure that they will not be lost among all the other colours in the bathroom. Perfume your design by spreading a layer of pot pourri over the top of the dry foam in which your flowers are arranged, or put a drop of an essential oil or a pot-pourri reviver on to the back of some of the larger flowers.

❧ INVIGORATING MIX
The sharp pine and lemon fragrance of this elegant pot pourri (left) is softened by a gentle floral background of rose and lavender.

❧ POT POURRIS ❧

POT POURRIS MADE FOR THE BATHROOM look lovely when displayed on the windowsill or bathroom dresser. Try to recreate the perfume of your home-made bath sachets or soaps so that the scents enhance one another – there is nothing better than being surrounded by your favourite scent when you are soaking in a bath at the end of a busy day. If you prefer to take a quick, invigorating shower rather than a bath, try fresh citrus or spicy perfumes to wake you up along with your wash. Heady, exotic fragrances are wonderful in a large and luxurious bathroom. A small, utilitarian bathroom is best scented with lighter, floral fragrances. Recreate the seasons by using perfumes that evoke them – the warm days of summer will come flooding back as you inhale the fragrance of roses and lavender. Present your pot pourri in a container that is in keeping with the bathroom. Shells, old-fashioned chamber pots and pottery soap dishes are ideal choices. Make sure that your container complements the colours of your pot pourri and the décor of your bathroom.

PERFUMED SOAP

❀ INGREDIENTS: LAVENDER, MOCK ORANGE BLOSSOM, ROSES, ROSE PETALS AND STAR ANISE.

❀ INGREDIENTS: ANAPHALIS, BLUEBELLS, LARKSPUR, ROSE BUDS AND ROSE PETALS.

❀ INGREDIENTS: ANAPHALIS (DYED PINK AND JADE), 'DE CAEN' ANEMONES, HYDRANGEA (DYED DARK GREEN) AND MALLOW.

❀ SPICY ROSE MIX
Sweet-smelling rose buds and spicy cinnamon sticks perfume this formal but delicate pot pourri (left).

❀ ORIENTAL MIX *Patchouli is used to enrich and enhance the sweet and heady oriental perfume of this pot pourri (left). It is a long-lasting mix as most of the ingredients are artificially coloured and therefore remain bright over a long period.*

❧ RECIPES ❧

FOR THE BATH

ROSE & ORANGE BATH OIL

75ml (2¹/₂fl oz) SUNFLOWER OIL
1 TABLESPOON HERBAL SHAMPOO
1 TABLESPOON ROSE OIL
1 TEASPOON ORANGE OIL

Bath Oils (p.103). Put sunflower oil, herbal shampoo and essential oils in a bottle, stopper and shake well. Leave for 2 weeks shaking daily. Use 1 tablespoon in the bath, pouring it under running hot water tap. VARIATION: To make pine bath oil use 1 tablespoon of pine oil and 1 teaspoon of lemon oil instead of the rose and orange oils.

GERANIUM & OAKMOSS TOILET VINEGAR

500ml (1pt) CIDER VINEGAR
(PREFERABLY A PALE ONE)
500ml (1pt) SPRING OR PURIFIED WATER
90g (3oz) FRESH GERANIUM
(PELARGONIUM) LEAVES
30g (1oz) OAKMOSS
4 DROPS GERANIUM OIL

Toilet Vinegar (p.103). Put geranium leaves and oakmoss in a container. Mix vinegar and water and heat to just below boiling point then pour over geranium leaves and oakmoss. Seal container with cling film and leave to infuse for 24 hours. Strain, add essential oils, bottle and cork. Shake well. Use about 1 cupful in the bath or dab on the body. Shake bottle before use.

FLORAL BUBBLE BATH

250ml (¹/₂pt) ORGANIC WASHING LIQUID
250ml (¹/₂pt) PURIFIED WATER
2 TEASPOONS ANY FLORAL ESSENTIAL OIL
2 DROPS FOOD COLOURING (OPTIONAL)

Bubble Baths (p.102). Mix organic washing liquid with purified water. Add essential oils and food colouring and mix well. Bottle. Use 1 tablespoon per bath. VARIATION: Substitute 2 teaspoons of clove oil for the floral oil for a spicy bubble bath.

❁ LARGE POSY
This lavender- and rose-scented posy is lovely in the bathroom.

BATH BAGS

60g (2oz) DRIED FLOWERS
30g (1oz) LAVENDER (OPTIONAL)
15g (¹/₂oz) ROLLED OATS
GRATED RIND OF ¹/₂ A LEMON

Bath Bags (pp.102-3). Put the mixed ingredients in small, cotton bags. Lavender enhances the perfume; oats make the water creamy.

FOR THE BODY

DRY SHAMPOO

120g (4oz) ORRIS ROOT POWDER
30g (1oz) UNPERFUMED TALC
4 DROPS ROSEMARY OIL

Dry Shampoo (p.103). Mix ingredients together thoroughly. Rub into hair, leave for 5 minutes and brush out.

ESSENTIAL OIL SOAP

250ml (¹/₂pt) Boiling Water
300g (10oz) Unscented Soap
6 Drops any Essential Oil
4 Drops Food Colouring

Essential Oil Soap (p.103).
Grate soap into a bowl, add other
ingredients and knead well. Leave to
harden. Place soap between cling
film, roll out to 2cm (³/₄in)
thick and cut tablets of soap with
a pastry cutter. Wrap in cling film
and leave for 24 hours. Remove
cling film and allow
soap to dry until hard.
Finally, polish with cotton
wool soaked in essential oil.

POT POURRIS FOR DISPLAY

SPICY ROSE MIX

500ml (1pt) Rose Buds
500ml (1pt) Rose Petals
60g (2oz) Lavender
30g (1oz) Orris Root Powder
2 Cinnamon Sticks
1 Teaspoon Cloves
3 Drops Geranium Oil
3 Drops Rose Oil
White Anaphalis & Blue
Larkspur Flowers to Decorate

The Spicy Rose Mix (pp.106-7)
is a dry pot pourri with a
fragrance of soft roses, spicy
cinnamon and cloves.

INVIGORATING MIX

500ml (1pt) Whole Roses
500ml (1pt) Mixed Lemon Balm, Lemon
Verbena & Chopped Pine Needles
30g (1oz) Lavender
30g (1oz) Fine-ground Gum Benzoin
Peel of a Lemon
2 Teaspoons Crushed Allspice Berries
6 Star Anise
4 Drops Pine Oil
2 Drops Lemon Oil
2 Drops Rose Oil
Mock Orange Blossom
to Decorate

The Invigorating Mix (p.106) is a
dry pot pourri in which several exciting
fragrances are blended together.

ORIENTAL MIX

1 litre (2pt) Mixed Pink- & Jade-dyed
Anaphalis, Dark Green-sprayed
Hydrangea Flowers & Black
Mallow Flowers
30g (1oz) Scented Geranium
(Pelargonium) Leaves
30g (1oz) Orris Root Powder
2 Teaspoons Cinnamon Powder
¹/₂ Teaspoon Cloves
4 Drops Narcissus Oil
(or any heady floral oil)
2 Drops Ylang Ylang Oil
1 Drop Patchouli Oil
'De Caen' Anemones & Purple
Statice to Decorate

The Oriental Mix (p.107) is a sweet
colourful dry pot pourri.

POT POURRIS FOR SACHETS

CITRUS & FLORAL MIX

250ml (¹/₂pt) Rose Petals
250ml (¹/₂pt) Lavender
30g (1oz) Hyssop
Grated Rind of ¹/₂ an Orange
Grated Rind of ¹/₂ a Lemon
1 Teaspoon Grated Nutmeg
4 Drops Vetiver Oil
2 Drops Lavender Oil
2 Drops Rose Oil

The Sea Sachets (p.98) are stuffed with
this lovely floral dry pot pourri, which has
tangy orange and lemon overtones.

INSECT-DETERRENT MIX

500ml (1pt) Rosemary
500ml (1pt) Southernwood
30g (1oz) Lavender
30g (1oz) Fine-ground Gum Benzoin
60g (2oz) Cloves
2 Teaspoons Cinnamon Powder
4 Drops Rosemary Oil
2 Drops Lavender Oil

The Floral Squares (p.99) are filled
with this dry pot pourri.

ORIENTAL JASMINE MIX

500ml (1pt) Jasmine Flowers
& Rose Petals
500ml (1pt) Lavender
30g (1oz) Fine-ground Gum Benzoin
30g (1oz) Crumbled Cinnamon
30g (1oz) Vetiver
Grated Rind of an Orange
1 Crumbled Star Anise
¹/₄ Chopped Vanilla Pod
4 Drops Jasmine Oil
4 Drops Lavender Oil
2 Drops Ylang Ylang Oil

The Blue Belles and the Ruby
Sachet (p.98) contain this mix.

HEADY LEMON MIX

500ml (1pt) Carnations
500ml (1pt) Lemon Verbena
60g (2oz) Basil
30g (1oz) Orris Root Powder
2 Tonquin Beans
¹/₂ Chopped Vanilla Pod
4 Drops Carnation Oil
2 Drops Lemon Oil
2 Drops Patchouli Oil

The Swinging Scent Sachets
(p.98) are filled with this
dry pot pourri.

BATH
OIL

BASIC TECHNIQUES

THE TECHNIQUES USED to make all the fragrant delights in this book are quite simple to follow and, once you have mastered them you can become more ambitious in the things you create. It is best to begin by learning how to make both dry and moist pot pourris, for, in doing so, you will understand the fundamental rules of creating and holding a fragrance. Pot pourri consists of five main groups of elements. First come the dried botanicals that form the bulk of the mix. In a dry pot pourri these might be rose petals or other scented petals or flowers, leaves, roots, seeds or woods; sometimes this group consists of dried botanicals that are attractive but not scented. In a moist pot pourri rose petals are cured with salt (and possibly brown sugar and brandy too). The resulting "stock pot" makes up the first group of botanicals. Second come the complementary sweet herbs. Usually just lavender is used although rosemary and other herbs can be included. Third come the fixatives. I have used mainly orris root powder or fine-ground gum benzoin. Fixatives are essential for holding the fragrance and without them the pot pourri quickly loses its scent. Fourth come the spices which add a subtle and interesting depth to the bouquet of the mix. Finally come the essential oils, the perfume of which dominates the pot pourri. Essential oils are concentrated perfumes extracted from aromatic plant materials. You will also need some lovely whole flowers and leaves, and possibly some whole spices, in order to decorate the whole mix. Scented colognes, essences, waters and oils are made by immersing fragrant plant materials in alcohol, vinegar or oil, this extracts the perfume from them.

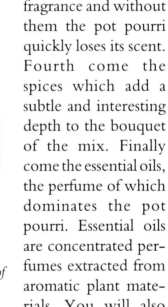

✿ EXTRACTING PERFUMES *Drying leaves and flowers (left) or making scented oils (above) are just two ways of using the fragrant elements in plants.*

❧ FRESH FLOWERS ❧

BRIGHTEN AND PERFUME any
room in the house by
decorating it with fresh, scented
flowers and aromatic greenery.

Gather the fragrant plant
materials when the sun has dried
the dew on them but has not yet
made the delicate flowers wilt:
this is usually around midday.
Choose flowers and leaves that
are in good condition; if they
are damaged they will quickly
deteriorate and you will have
to renew the display.

Start by making a simple,
fan-shaped arrangement,
such as the one shown
here, and then experiment
with other shapes as your
confidence grows.

MAKING A FAN-SHAPED ARRANGEMENT

1 *Gather the tools and ingredients you
need: a knife to cut the wet foam, scissors
or secateurs to trim stems and leaves, an
attractive container and the plant materials.*

2 *Shape the foam to fit the container. Place
it inside and moisten it well. Starting from
the centre back, make a basic fan shape.
Then fill out towards the front.*

❀ WINTER GREENERY
*This display of scented
evergreens, with fragrant
jonquils and daphne to
provide colour, is arranged
in a classic fan shape.*

✤ DRIED FLOWERS ✤

Flowers can be dried and used in dried-flower designs and pot pourris. A simple way to dry them is to remove most of the leaves, make a bunch – varying the height of the flowerheads – and hang it upside–down in a warm, dry, shady place. Drying with silica gel is more complicated but the flowers keep their colours better.

❋ HANG-DRYING *Bunches of flowers hung in a warm, shady place make a lovely display.*

DRYING WITH SILICA GEL

1 *Fill the bottom of an airtight container with 2cm (1in) of silica gel. With scissors or secateurs, remove the flowerheads carefully. Whole sprays of flowers may also be dried.*

2 *If you plan to add wire stems, insert a pin in the back of each flower. Place them face-up in the container. (Flat flowers, such as daisies, may be placed face-down.)*

3 *Sprinkle silica gel between the petals and over the flowers until they are covered with 2cm (1in) of gel. Remove the flowers in 3 to 4 days or when they are crispy dry.*

❧ PRESSED FLOWERS ❧

PRESSED PLANT MATERIALS can be used in many ways – to make collages and posters, to decorate old bottles and jars, and to embellish cards, notepaper, gift tags and bookmarks.

Almost any plant material – including mosses, seedheads and berries – can be pressed. The material you use must be in good condition and should not be picked when wet.

Gather the plant material as it becomes available. Arrange materials of similar thickness in each layer to ensure an even pressure is applied, but include a variety of plants so that you have plenty of choice when making your design.

For the best results dry the plant material quickly. Do this by placing three sheets of folded, empty, recycled paper between the paper that contains the pressed plant materials and replace this paper regularly. The paper can be dried and reused.

When it is dry and crisp – after about two weeks – remove the material from the press and store it between sheets of recycled paper in a dry place so that it does not go mouldy.

PRESSING FLOWERS

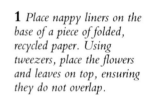

1 *Place nappy liners on the base of a piece of folded, recycled paper. Using tweezers, place the flowers and leaves on top, ensuring they do not overlap.*

2 *Cover with more nappy liners, fold over the paper and place in the press. When it is full, screw the press down firmly.*

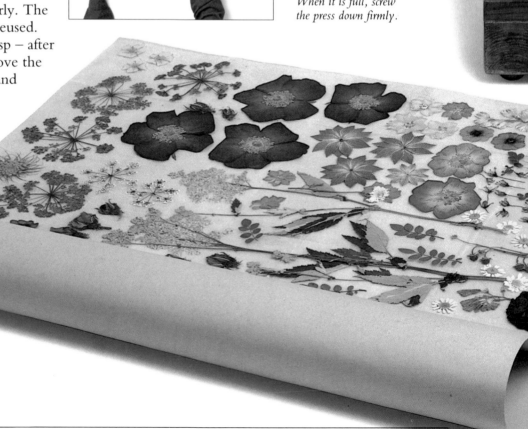

❀ FLOWER PRESS *This large press is ideal for those wishing to press a large amount of material. Smaller presses are available for the beginner.*

❀ PRESSED-FLOWER LAYER *These beautiful pressed flowers and leaves are ready to be used in a design.*

❧ POT POURRI ☙

THERE ARE TWO BASIC WAYS of making pot pourri: the dry method and the moist method.

Dry pot pourris are quick and easy to make and very attractive. Moist pot pourris are more highly scented than dry pot pourris and, although less attractive, can be stored in pretty containers that are perforated to allow the fragrance to escape. They are prepared in two stages: the making of the stock-pot, which provides the intense scent, and the mixing of the stock-pot with the dry ingredients.

MAKING A MOIST POT POURRI

1 *Separate the rose petals and leave to dry for 2 days. Fill an airtight jar with petals in $1^{1}/_{2}$ cm ($^{2}/_{3}$ in) layers, sprinkling each layer with salt (if desired, also sprinkle with brown sugar and drops of brandy). Continue adding more petals as they become available over a season, pressing each layer down well.*

2 *Leave to cure for 2 months, draining off excess liquid, if necessary. Crumble the matured "stock-pot" into a bowl that contains the other ingredients. Store the resulting moist pot pourri in an airtight jar for 3 weeks. Remove and display in an attractive perforated container.*

❀ DRY POT POURRI *Decorate the finished dry pot pourri with dried, whole flowers.*

❀ **FOR A MOIST POT POURRI YOU WILL NEED**: A SUPPLY OF ROSE PETALS, BROWN SUGAR, BRANDY, COARSE SALT.

❀ **FOR A DRY POT POURRI YOU WILL NEED**: 1 litre (2pt) DRIED FLOWERS, LEAVES, ROOTS OR SEEDS, 30g (1oz) LAVENDER, 30g (1oz) ORRIS ROOT POWDER, 1 TEASPOON CINNAMON POWDER, 6 DROPS OF ESSENTIAL OIL.

MAKING A DRY POT POURRI

1 *Place fixatives, such as orris root powder or ground gum benzoin, and any powdered spices in a bowl, add essential oils and rub the mix between fingers until well blended.*

2 *Blend the remaining dry ingredients together in a large bowl. Then add the combined fixatives and essential oils and stir the mixture well, using a wooden spoon.*

3 *Store the mixture in an airtight container or sealed plastic bag for 4-6 weeks. Remove, place in an attractive bowl or dish and decorate the top with whole dried flowers.*

SCENTED PAPER

SCENTED STATIONERY is simple to make and adds a special touch to your correspondence. Make stationery using art paper, tearing it by hand to give it an attractive edge, or decorate shop-bought paper. Scent the paper by storing it with a sachet of pot pourri for four weeks. Perfume and protect pressed-flower designs on bookmarks, gift tags and cards by painting them with melted, scented wax.

TEARING & SCENTING PAPER

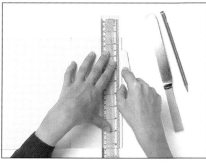

1 *Use a ruler to draw a line where you wish to tear the paper. Score line with a knife, fold and press along the fold. Turn paper over and repeat. Tear paper along the fold.*

2 *Staple together 2 tissues or nappy liners on 3 sides to make a sachet. Fill it with pot pourri and staple the final edge. Place the sachet and paper in a plastic bag and seal.*

❀ PAPER ARRAY *A wide variety of stationery can be made at home.*

❀ BLUE PAPER *Stored in a plastic bag with a pot-pourri sachet, this paper is imbued with scent.*

❧ DECORATED CANDLES ❧

P LAIN, WHITE DOMESTIC CANDLES are very attractive when they are decorated with pressed herbs and flowers. They are also the easiest candles to work with and are therefore suitable for the beginner to decorate. Select tall, spiky fronds or long flowerheads to decorate candles and avoid using bulky plant material, such as berries, as it is a potential fire hazard.

Take great care when you work with wax. Remember that melted wax is highly flammable, so always use a low heat, and a deep, preferably double, saucepan. Do not allow the wax to touch the skin as it will cause painful burning.

After some practice, try decorating coloured, tapering candles and, eventually, try making your own candles. Beeswax candles can be bought in any craft shop.

1 *In a deep or double saucepan, gently melt wax over a low heat. Hold the candle by the wick and dip it into the wax. Allow to cool for 10 minutes and dip again.*

❀ **FOR DECORATING DOMESTIC CANDLES YOU WILL NEED:** ENOUGH WAX TO COVER THE CANDLE WHEN IT IS DIPPED INTO THE SAUCEPAN, 6 DROPS OF WAX PERFUME OR ESSENTIAL OIL FOR EVERY 360g (12OZ) OF WAX, A SELECTION OF PRESSED FLOWERS & HERBS.

❀ **SCENTED CANDLES** *Although difficult for the beginner, with practice most of these candles can be made at home.*

2 *When the candle is cool place the pressed herbs or flowers in position on it. Brush melted wax over the decoration to hold it in place and leave to cool for 10 minutes.*

3 *Dip the whole candle in the melted wax again to seal the decoration on the candle. Allow to cool completely and then polish the surface with a soft cloth or tissue.*

❀ CITRUS POMANDER
The tangy scent of a
citrus pomander
is especially lovely
in the kitchen.

❀ **FOR A FLORAL POMANDER YOU
WILL NEED:** A SPHERE OF DRY FOAM,
60g (2oz) OF LAVENDER FLOWERS,
A GOOD SELECTION OF SCENTED,
DRIED FLOWERS, GLUE, RIBBON.

❀ **FOR A CITRUS POMANDER YOU
WILL NEED:** A CITRUS FRUIT,
CLOVES, 30g (1oz) ORRIS ROOT
POWDER, 30g (1oz) CINNAMON
POWDER, 4 DROPS OF A TANGY
ESSENTIAL OIL, TAPE, RIBBON,
PINS, BEADS, A KNITTING NEEDLE.

❀ FLORAL
POMANDER
Brighten and
scent any
room with a
floral pomander.

⚜ POMANDERS ⚜

THERE ARE TWO basic types
of pomander: the citrus
pomander – a citrus fruit
decorated with cloves – and
the floral pomander – a sphere
of dry foam decorated with
dried flowers. Although time-
consuming, neither type is
difficult to learn how to
make and the end result is
a lovely, scented decoration.

MAKING A FLORAL POMANDER

1 *Using a paintbrush, dab patches of glue
on to the dry foam then carefully roll it in
the lavender flowers.*

2 *Using tweezers, pick up a dried flower,
dip the back into glue, then place in position.
Add flowers of a kind in small groups.*

MAKING A CITRUS POMANDER

1 *Divide the fruit into quarters with tape.
Starting next to the tape, working into the
centre of each quarter, make holes ³/₄ cm
(¹/₃ in) apart. Place a clove in each hole.*

2 *Remove tape and put the pomander in a
bag containing a mixture of cinnamon, orris
root and essential oil. Shake well, remove,
brush off excess and wrap in tissue paper.*

3 *Leave in a dry place for 2 to 3 weeks.
Remove from tissue. Decorate with ribbon
and beads. (Omit step 2 should you wish
to have a purely citrus-scented pomander.)*

❧ DECORATIONS ❧

ONE OF THE MOST BEAUTIFUL and effective ways of using dried flowers is in a three-dimensional design. Such a decoration looks wonderful displayed in the centre of a table but, of course, you can place them on many other flat surfaces to great effect.

The basic steps to follow are straightforward but the finished arrangement can be as intricate as you wish. Begin with a simple design and then experiment with more ambitious ideas.

3 *When the moss is in place, turn over the card and glue a border of lacy flowers on the underside. They should extend over the edge so that they are visible from the right side.*

MAKING A CENTREPIECE

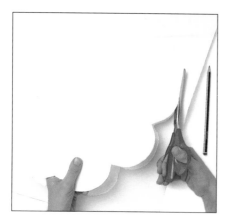

1 *With a pencil, mark your design on to watercolour paper or white card. Use a template if you wish. Then cut carefully around the shape, using sharp scissors.*

4 *Trim any stalks off the flowers. Starting from the outside, gradually work inwards, gluing the flowers on to the moss in informal rows that follow the shape of the card.*

2 *Cover the whole of the shape with moss. Pick up the pieces of moss with tweezers, dip the backs into a saucer of glue and then stick them in place on the card.*

5 *Add scent by carefully dripping essential oil followed by oil of cloves into the centre of a few of the flowers. Oil of cloves is a fixative, so the perfume will be long-lasting.*

❧ TOILETRIES ❧

COSMETIC CREAMS, perfumes, soaps, shampoos, bath oils and toilet waters are very simple to make in your own home. Most of the ingredients involved are natural and you can scent the products with your favourite fragrances. Food colouring can be added to alcohol- or vinegar-based toiletries to make them more visually attractive.

❀ **FOR JONQUIL COLOGNE YOU WILL NEED:** 500ml (1pt) VODKA, A SUPPLY OF FRESH, HIGHLY PERFUMED JONQUILS, 2 DROPS OF FOOD COLOURING.

❀ **FOR BODY OIL YOU WILL NEED:** 50ml (1½ fl oz) ALMOND OIL, 10 DROPS OF ANY FLORAL ESSENTIAL OIL.

✿ SCENTED DELIGHTS
*All these cosmetics
and toiletries can be
made at home.*

MAKING JONQUIL COLOGNE

1 *Pour in enough vodka to reach the shoulders of a bottle. Push the flowers into the bottle until the liquid is full. Cork and leave for 10 days, gently shaking daily.*

2 *Strain the liquid and replace the flowers with new ones. Repeat the whole process 3 times then bottle, add colouring and cork. Use glue to attach dried-flower decorations.*

MAKING BODY OIL

This is one of the easiest toiletries to make. Pour almond oil into a bottle, add essential oil, place the stopper in the bottle and shake well. The oil is now ready to use.

❧ CUSHIONS & SACHETS ❧

LARGE, SCENTED CUSHIONS are easy to make and, once you have mastered the basic sewing techniques, smaller, more intricate, fragrant sachets will be well within your abilities.

Cushion covers are best made from materials that can be removed and washed, especially if the cushions will be in frequent use. Sachets are usually used purely as decoration so they can be made of more delicate materials, such as ribbon and lace.

❀ FOR SACHETS & CUSHIONS YOU WILL NEED: SCISSORS, PINS, NEEDLE, THREAD, CLOTH, LACE, RIBBON, WADDING, POT POURRI.

MAKING A CUSHION

1 *Use a template to cut out 6 pieces of 120g (4oz), flame-proof wadding. The shape should be 1cm (¹/₂ in) smaller all-round than the cover you intend to use.*

2 *Holding or pinning the 6 pieces of wadding together, sew around 3 sides of the shape, to make an envelope. (If the shape is round, leave a portion of the edge unsewn.)*

3 *Fill the wadding envelope with a highly scented pot pourri. Sew the final edge together. Cut out and sew around 3 sides of the material you wish to use as a cover.*

❀ CUSHIONS
*Large, scented
cushions require
more sewing than
sachets but are less
fiddly to make.*

❀ BUTTERFLIES
*Sachets can be any
shape. These butterflies
are simple to make and
quite charming.*

4 *Ease the envelope of wadding into the
cushion cover and sew up the final edge.
(Use poppers or a zip if you wish to be
able to remove the filling at a later date.)*

❧ SUPPLIERS ❧

SPICES, DRIED FLOWERS & HERBS, FIXATIVES & OILS

PIERCE A. ARNOLD & SON LTD
(wholesale only)
12 Park Road
Hackbridge
Wallington
Surrey SM6 7ES

CARLEY & CO
34/36 St Austell Street
Truro
Cornwall TR1 1SE

CHATTELS
53 Chalk Farm Road
London NW1 8AN

CULPEPPER LTD
21 Bruton Street
London W1X 7DA

FLORIS
89 Jermyn Street
London SW1 6JH

NATURAL CHOICE
HEALTH FOODS
16 High Street
Falmouth
Cornwall

HANDMADE PAPER

THE TWO RIVERS
PAPER COMPANY
Rosebank Mill
Stubbin, Nr Bury
Lancashire

DRYING CRYSTALS & FLORA-SEAL

M. F. CRYSTALS
77 Bulbridge Road
Wilton, Salisbury
Wiltshire SP2 0LE
(SAE please)

FABRICS

LIBERTY
Regent Street
London W1R 6AH

WILDFLOWER PLANTS & SEEDS

JOHN CHAMBERS
15 Westleigh Road
Barton Seagrave
Kettering
Northamptonshire
NN15 5AJ

LANDLIFE WILD
FLOWERS LTD
The Old Police
Station
Lark Lane
Liverpool L17 8UU

NPK LANDSCAPE
ARCHITECTS
542 Parrs Wood Road
East Didsbury
Manchester M20 0QA

SUFFOLK HERBS LTD
Sawyer's Farm
Little Cornard
Sudbury
Suffolk CO10 0NY

CERAMIC POTS & BOWLS

DEBBIE PROSSER
Penhalvean Farm
Penhalvean
Stithians
Truro

FRESH & DRIED FLOWERS, BASKETS & CONTAINERS

JACKIE PHILLIPS
FLOWERS
5 The Moor
Falmouth
Cornwall

HAND-DYED SILK THREADS

THE PRIDEAUX
COLLECTION
Towan Textiles Workshop
Trevilla
Feoch
Truro
Cornwall TR3 6QT

❀ STORAGE JARS *These lovely jars contain pot pourri. When put on display, the lids are removed to allow the fragrance to escape.*

✦ CONSERVATION OF WILD PLANTS ✦

THROUGH MY LOVE of gardening and my interest in the historical significance of our wild and cultivated plants, has grown an awareness of the threat that we pose to the survival of our environment. There must now be some redress to the balance of the intricate and fragile equilibrium of the natural world. Everyone can make some contribution towards this and I hope that the contents of this book will encourage all those who read it to experiment with alternative ways of freshening and sweetening their homes. I also hope that it will stimulate an interest in natural beauty preparations. All these fragrant delights are bio-degradable and pose no threat to the atmosphere.

Most of the wild and cultivated plants that I use in my recipes are grown and gathered from my own garden. In my tamed wilderness, wildlings grow cheek by jowl with their cultivated cousins and the garden is a haven for the prolific Cornish wildlife. Help to protect the environment by trying to grow wild species in your garden – many seed merchants sell wild plant seed and there are specialist nurseries from whom you can buy wild plants.

If you do gather wild flowers never pick them from a plant that has no companions, always leave some flowers to set seed and never pick more flowers than you need. I believe that we should all grow some wild plants in our gardens for by so doing we can at least ensure their perpetuation. Many wild plants are now protected and should under no circumstances be touched. A list of these is available from Department of the Environment, Tollgate House, Houlton Street, Bristol BS2 9DJ.

✦ POISONOUS PLANTS ✦

TAKE GREAT CARE in gathering plants, flowers, berries and seeds. Often, those that appear to be the brightest and most attractive are, in fact, poisonous. The following is a list of the more common poisonous berries. Do **not** use them in your preparations. No matter how beautiful they are, it is not worth the risk.

Common Name	Latin Name	Common Name	Latin Name
Black Locust	Robinia pseudoacacia	Mayapple, mandrake	Podophyllum peltatum
Castor-bean	Ricinus communis	Poison ivy	Rhus radicans
Common moonseed	Menispermum canadense	Poison sumac	Rhus vernix
Deadly nightshade	Solanum dulcamara	Pokeweed	Phytolacca americana
English ivy	Hedera helix	Spindle tree	Euonymus europaea
February daphne	Daphne mezereum	Wisteria	Wisteria spp.
Golden-chain	Laburnum anagyroides	Yews	Taxus spp.

❧ Index ❧

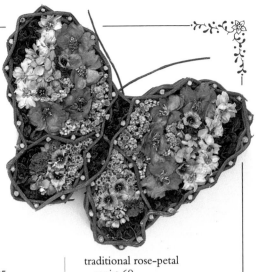

☙ ACKNOWLEDGMENTS ❧

The author would like to thank all those at Dorling Kindersley who have worked so hard on this book. Jo Weeks, my editor, for her quiet enthusiasm and hard work; Caroline Mulvin, the designer, for her artistic contribution; Kate Grant for collecting my work and transporting it to London with such care, and Jane Laing and Alex Arthur for overseeing the project. Finally, a special thank you to my family, who always keep me going in moments of self doubt.

Dorling Kindersley would like to thank the following:

Lunn Antiques, New King's Road, London for the lace pillow cases and nightdress case (pp.72-3), Owen Owen, Richmond, Surrey and The Reject China Shop, Regent Street, London for assorted crockery and cutlery. Germana Arthur for the linen press (p.56) and sundries kindly lent throughout the book, Lucinda and Emma Ganderton for assorted decorative bottles (pp. 76-7, 102-3, 111),

Valerie and Heather Janitch for the lavender bundles (p.70), Deirdre and Mark Moloney for their teddy (p.86), Dodie Strasser for the easel (pp.28-9) and Hopscotch Props for the cot (p.86). Also thanks to Susan Thompson and Heather Dewhurst for editorial help, Pauline Bayne for the illustrations, Peter Moloney for the index, Kate Grant for keying-in and Maryann Rogers for help with production.